FASHIONED
to
Reign

Other Books and Materials by Kris Vallotton

Developing a Supernatural Lifestyle:
A Practical Guide to a Life of Signs, Wonders, and Miracles

God's Most Beautiful Creation
(a six-part DVD or CD teaching series on women)

Heavy Rain: Renew the Church,
Transform the World

Moral Revolution:
The Naked Truth about Sexual Purity

Outrageous Courage:
What God Can Do with Raw Obedience and Radical Faith
(the Tracy Evans story; co-authored with Jason Vallotton)

School of the Prophets:
Advanced Training for Prophetic Ministry
(book, workbook, leader's guide and video segments available,
or an all-inclusive curriculum kit)

Spirit Wars:
Winning the Invisible Battle against Sin and the Enemy
(book, workbook, leader's guide and video segments available,
or an all-inclusive curriculum kit)

The Supernatural Power of Forgiveness:
Discover How to Escape Your Prison of Pain and Unlock a Life of Freedom
(co-authored with Jason Vallotton)

The Supernatural Ways of Royalty:
Discovering Your Rights and Privileges of Being a Son or Daughter of God
(co-authored with Bill Johnson)

Basic Training for the Supernatural Ways of Royalty
(workbook)

Basic Training for the Prophetic Ministry
(workbook)

FASHIONED to Reign

Empowering Women to Fulfill Their Divine Destiny

KRIS VALLOTTON

Chosen

a division of Baker Publishing Group
Minneapolis, Minnesota

Published by Chosen Books
11400 Hampshire Avenue South
Bloomington, Minnesota 55438
www.chosenbooks.com

Chosen Books is a division of
Baker Publishing Group, Grand Rapids, Michigan

Printed in the United States of America

ISBN 978-0-8007-9608-2 (pbk.)

Cover design by Dan Pitts

14 15 16 17 18 19 20   7 6 5 4 3 2 1

Contents

It's Time to Incite a Revolution!

I wrote the book *Fashioned to Reign: Empowering Women to Fulfill Their Divine Destiny* because I saw that it was time to incite a revolution in the Church. Far too many female believers are prohibited from fulfilling their divine destinies by prejudice and poor theology. Those each have been used for far too long to "keep women in their place" in the Church. I also do not believe that the "place" we have assigned to women is the place God had in mind when He created womankind. Nor is it the place they have been given according to Scripture.

The Scriptures that refer to women and their place in the Church can open up a world of debate. Believe me, I know! I have been involved in plenty of that debate. Every day, I wake up amazed at the number of Christian leaders who do not believe that women are as qualified, called or gifted as men to lead in the Church. And the way in which these limiting leaders use Scripture to back up that belief also amazes me. The truths of Scripture are not up for debate, but we had better make sure that we are accurate in our interpretations before we use them to legislate and limit people's lives.

I no longer want poor theology to limit what my wife, daughters and granddaughters (not to mention my numerous spiritual daughters) can accomplish for God. I no longer want these beautiful women of God to wake up every day to face the kind of discrimination that keeps them from becoming everything God meant for them to be. It is not right, and it does untold damage to the Church's efforts to fulfill the Great Commission.

On the other hand, when we empower women to do what God has gifted and called them to do, the results are out of this world, literally. They are of eternal consequence. When women step up into their rightful place alongside men in both the Church and in society at large, it is then that we begin to see the glory of God cover the earth as waters cover the sea. I like to say, and I will show from Scripture, that Jesus founded the first Women's Liberation Movement. He knew what He was doing!

I did not write *Fashioned to Reign* to quarrel with anyone about words or to provoke fruitless arguments. Scripture charges us "not to quarrel about words, which does no good, but only ruins the hearers" (2 Timothy 2:14 ESV). Rather, we are told, "Do your best to present yourself to God as one approved, a worker who has no need to be ashamed, rightly handling the word of truth" (verse 15 ESV). I have the utmost respect for those with a different perspective from mine who are determined to honor God by being true to His Word to the best of their understanding. I would not want them—or you—to do anything less. It would be a shame for any of us to become "culturally relevant" in any area of our lives at the expense of perverting the Word of God.

What I do ask of those who differ with me on the empowerment of women, however (and of you if you are in that group), is that they hear me out when it comes to the role of women as presented in Scripture. This goes beyond cultural relevance, to the very foundations of what we believe about why God made us male and female. Stay with me to the end. The chapters in my book and the sessions in this workbook build on one another and fit together like the pieces of a puzzle. Near the end of our time in this study, I think you will see a bigger picture emerge that will deepen your understanding of God's purpose and place for women.

One of my goals in writing *Fashioned to Reign* and putting together this curriculum was to do just as the verses I quoted say—to help believers rightly handle the word of truth, particularly in the area of a woman's role in the Kingdom. Through careful study and diligent scholarship, I present in these pages what I believe is solid evidence from Scripture that women are as qualified, called and gifted as men, and are heirs to the same promises that men have in Christ. My prayer is that through this material, you, too, will wake up to that realization, if you have not already. If you are female, I pray that you will be empowered to walk in your full destiny and God-given identity, unaffected by how the world sees you and who religious pressure says you should be.

It is my further hope and prayer that as all of us move through this *Fashioned to Reign* study together and learn more about what God created womankind to be, you will join me in inciting a revolution. For the sake of every woman serving in the Kingdom, I invite you to become a revolutionary!

Vallotton • *Fashioned to Reign*
IT'S TIME TO INCITE A REVOLUTION!

8

Be Encouraged and Empowered

How to Use This Curriculum

This workbook is divided into eight sessions that will take you deeper into the topic I explore in my book *Fashioned to Reign*—empowering women of God everywhere to fulfill their God-given destinies. Each session will take five days to go through, and each day lists different readings for you from Scripture and from the book. Each day also provides questions for you to answer that will help you think through what you are learning as you discover more about God's divine destiny for women.

Move through the daily readings at a thoughtful pace, praying that the Holy Spirit will become your teacher and "guide you into all truth" (John 16:13). Approach the questions with an open heart and an open ear, listening for the Holy Spirit's input and direction as you tackle the hard questions with me about the way we define and limit the role of women in the Church. We are about to take a hard look at whether we have been faithful to Scripture and to the heart of God in our definition of that role.

At the end of each session, there is also a life application that helps you take what you learned in that session and apply it to your life in a specific, concrete way. I believe that knowledge is valuable and that increasing our knowledge about spiritual things is important. I am a strong supporter of serious scholarship, and I helped found and currently oversee the Bethel School of Supernatural Ministry. But while educating ourselves about spiritual things is crucial, it can only take us so far, unless we take what we know and make application with it. To *know* something and to *do* something about it are two entirely different things. Application is an important part of any study—probably the most important part. I urge you to take concrete steps to apply what you are learning in this study by following through with each session's life application. (If you are part of a *Fashioned to Reign* study group, make sure to implement the life applications before your group meetings so that you can discuss the results.)

Note that I did not put together the readings, questions and life applications in this workbook as a means of adding to your daily busywork. We all have enough busywork! I designed this workbook so that you can skip one day and come back the next if needed, or do two days at a time and still get through each session in about a week. Each day's readings and questions should take only twenty or thirty minutes of your time, and I think you will find that the results will be well worth it.

Keep in mind that as with any curriculum, you will get out of this study what you put into it. Stay faithful in doing the daily lessons, and stick with me from beginning to end. If you will do that, I believe the results will encourage and empower all of us, men and women alike, as together we seek to bring the Good News of God's Kingdom to the world.

While you can use the *Fashioned to Reign* book and workbook at home to study these things on your own, you will also see that there is a video guide at the end of each workbook section. Those fill-in-the-blank guides are included because I have recorded a series of eight video segments that go along with these materials. In the video segments, which are geared for use in a small group setting, I have added a lot more depth and clarification to each section. You can purchase and view the videos yourself, which will greatly enhance what you gain from this study. They were designed, however, to promote fellowship with other believers as you walk through this study together and pray for and encourage each other. It is ideal to become part of a group that will use the *Fashioned to Reign* book, workbook and video segments as tools to inform and educate everyone in the group and to foster discussion about how each of you can apply what you are learning most effectively. I urge you to join a *Fashioned to Reign* study group if one is available at your church or somewhere nearby. If you cannot find such a group, you can host one. A *Fashioned to Reign Curriculum Kit* for group leaders is also available to help you do just that.

"Fashioned" by God

For thousands of years, forces that are out to destroy the dignity, glory and self-respect of the human race have been at work in our world. The brunt force of this battle predominantly has been executed against women. It is a battle that puts the sexes at war with each other as each sex creates standards from its own strengths that demean the other. The majority of the contention has involved men requiring women to measure up to masculine standards, while ignoring the superior strengths of feminine virtues . . .

Fashioned to Reign, page 39

Day 1

Matriarchs Needed

There is no longer Jew or Gentile, slave or free, male and female.
For you are all one in Christ Jesus.

Galatians 3:28

At a time when matriarchs are needed to step up alongside patriarchs in every area of society and the Church and contribute the best of what they have to offer, it disturbs me that so many believers subscribe to a theology that proactively uses the Bible to disqualify women from key leadership roles. What a loss to society and the Church!

Such disempowering theology is not only illogical; it is also unscriptural. (I will talk a lot more about that statement as we go along.) Socially and scripturally, women have a better track record in many ways than men. We men in the Church are shooting ourselves in the foot, so to speak, when we cripple a woman's ability to lead in areas where she is called and gifted to do so.

But *there* is the very point of contention—in what areas might a woman be called and gifted to lead, especially within the Church? Almost any man on the planet is delighted when a woman leads the way in cooking and cleaning at home and in caring for his children, and there is nothing wrong with those activities. They are vitally important to carrying on the human race. But the question of which gender is relegated to doing them is a whole different matter. I do not have a problem with women doing those things (or with men doing them, for that matter). I have a problem with women being limited by men to doing *only* those things. Based on what I see in Scripture, I think Jesus had a problem with that, too.

Clear back to the Genesis curse, the God-ordained role of women has been a point of contention. In *Fashioned to Reign*, we will look at several examples of women who were empowered, or sadly, in some cases were disempowered by virtue of their time and place in history. More importantly, however, we will look at just what it was that God ordained for His daughters to be doing and becoming in His Kingdom. It is time for the misinterpretations of His Word in that area to stop. Once again, I urge you to stay with me throughout this study as we do our best to diligently and accurately understand the Scriptures and to hear God's heart on this topic.

- Today's Scripture reading: Galatians 3:23–29
- Today's reading from *Fashioned to Reign*: pages 15–22

— *Questions to Consider* —

1. In the Foreword to *Fashioned to Reign*, Pastor Jack Hayford notes that strained interpretations of the Bible can cause people to resist the simplicity and wholeness that God's Word presents. What do you think motivates people to complicate the Scriptures?

   Strained interpretations – Resisting Simplicity and wholeness that God's presents.

2. In the book's Acknowledgments, I mention some people who have greatly enlarged my understanding of the role of women. Who has influenced your beliefs in this area? How have they done so?

   My dear friend Victory who led me to the Lord. Quoting scriptures and teaching God's word to me.

3. In today's reading from the book, I give four basic reasons why I believe men and women are not empowered equally. Give an example of how any one of those reasons has caused role issues or leadership problems for you or for a woman you know. (See *Fashioned to Reign* page 21.)

   People missunderstand the place the Lord has given them.

4. Even at this early stage, just from reading what I have expressed in my Introduction, you can probably tell if your beliefs about the empowerment of women align with mine or are different. If your beliefs are different from mine, what is drawing you to take part in

this study? Will you stay with it to the end, as I have requested? Will you remain open to changing your perspective?

My feelings are like his
Yes I will. Yes I will Remain
open to change

Day 2

Identifying with Adam

For since by a man came death, by a man also came the resurrection of the dead. For as in Adam all die, so also in Christ all will be made alive.

1 Corinthians 15:21–22

The first man, Adam, went through some agony and ecstasy, only in the opposite order. He was ecstatic during his time in the Garden of Eden. He named the animals one by one and no suitable helper was found for him, so God created the woman whom he called Eve. She was bone of his bone and flesh of his flesh, and he instantly identified with her as a part of himself. What a joyful story!

Then came the agony: the serpent's machinations and Eve's tasting of the forbidden fruit, followed by Adam's tasting of it. Adam and Eve's newfound and terrifying knowledge of good and evil, and their shame and guilt at disobeying God. The consequences of the curse that fell upon them and their expulsion from the beautiful Garden. What a sad story—the saddest story ever told.

I can identify with Adam. In fact, I think you will find today's reading in the book interesting as I identify with Adam in a unique way. I take you with me into his story the way I suddenly imagined it one day as I was reading the creation account. (Granted, I have a vivid imagination, as you are about to find out.)

Let me stress again, as I do in the book itself, that I make no claims that the Holy Spirit inspired the Adam narrative I wrote. But I will say that my unique journey into Adam's story gave me a new perspective on what it might have been like for Adam and Eve at the dawning of creation. It moved me to laughter and tears. It was almost like being there . . .

I hope the story will do the same for you as I share it with you.

- Today's Scripture reading: 1 Corinthians 15:20–49
- Today's reading from *Fashioned to Reign*: pages 23–37

— Questions to Consider —

1. Now that you have read my imaginative story about Adam, what do you think of it? Even though you may not think everything happened exactly as I imagined it, what was your favorite part of the story? Why?

   When God made the animals and had Adam name them.

2. What do you think of the conversation between God and Adam about Adam's loneliness? Why didn't any of the animals satisfy his loneliness? (See *Fashioned to Reign* pages 24–25.) Do you know any people who feel that the companionship of animals is all that they need?

   That the animals could only satisfy his loneliness for so long. They were not like him, couldn't talk to them. No I don't.

3. In my story, Adam is both captivated and confused by Eve as he gets to know her and begins to understand how different she is from him. Name a few ways in which men and women are still captivated and confused by each other. (This question should be really easy!)

   They each take care of each other n they are captivated by their beauty. They each have their own feelings but cannot understand these feelings each one has.

4. What does it mean to say that Adam and Even chose to change masters at the Fall? How did their relationship with each other also change? (See Adam's "explanation" on page 35 of *Fashioned to Reign*.)

   They ate of the forbidden tree and n became followers of Satan, Adam ruled over Eve.

5. Do you imagine, as I do, that Adam and Eve often wondered how humankind might be restored back to the Garden—or at least back to their Garden relationship with God and each other? What was God's answer for that hope and longing? (See *Fashioned to Reign* page 37.)

I imagine after loosing that relation with God they often thought of getting it back. He said nothing but let them wonder & wait for the rejoicing of the children of God.

6. Have you ever identified so closely with someone in Scripture that you imagined the details of that person's story and the events surrounding his or her life the way I did with Adam? Who was it you identified with? What effect did putting yourself in that person's place, so to speak, have on you?

Not so completely as Adam & God. The person that led me to the Lord. When she revealed her story I felt her pain and troubles

Day 3

After the God Kind

"Let Us make man in Our image, according to Our likeness. . . ."
God created man in His own image, in the image of God He
created him; male and female He created them.

Genesis 1:26–27

Science intrigues me. I find the lives and discoveries of many scientists fascinating, and I see no reason why my faith and my love of science should be incompatible. There are some areas of science, however, where it becomes necessary to draw the line. From my perspective, one of the biggest of those areas is Darwinism. In today's book reading, I explain why. Whatever your take is on evolution, hear me out as you read today's pages in *Fashioned to Reign*.

Darwin's advocacy of *inner species* evolution forms the crux of my problem with him. To say that one single organism evolved into all the species on the planet dismantles the very foundation of our identity as children of God. (Not to mention that it stands in direct opposition to Genesis 1's creation account.) We were created in the image and likeness of God our Father. We were made after *His* kind—not that we are gods, but we were created to be godlike in our behavior and love for each other. In other words, we live to follow the example of our Daddy and His Son and to become like them.

Darwin's theories have had the net result of devaluing and disgracing humanity for decades. But to say that we were made after the God kind, not the amoeba kind, puts a whole different value on the human race. I think we have to get that straight to begin with to truly value ourselves and each other. Then we can move on from there into a proper valuation of the female kind.

- Today's Scripture reading: Genesis 1; Romans 8:14–25
- Today's reading from *Fashioned to Reign*: pages 39–42

Questions to Consider

1. What does it mean to say that Charles Darwin gave the world the excuse it needed to "live like hell and not have to answer to heaven"? (See *Fashioned to Reign* page 40.)

   There are no rules n they can live anyway they want to wich no fear of consequences.

2. Darwin's theory of evolution stated that *all* life on earth evolved from the *same kind*. How does the Genesis 1 phrase *after their kind* give us the polar-opposite perspective on the origin of life? (See *Fashioned to Reign* page 41.)

3. What does it do to people's mind-sets to believe that they are cosmic accidents with no eternal consequence rather than believing they are offspring of God with an earthly purpose and a heavenly destiny?

   They believe there is no God n there will be nothing when they augone.

Day 4

Two Halves of a Whole

This is now bone of my bones,
And flesh of my flesh;
She shall be called Woman,
Because she was taken out of Man.

Genesis 2:23

Genesis 1 tells us that God created humankind in His own image, male and female, and then He immediately commanded them to be fruitful and multiply. So far, so good. Genesis 2 tells us that God, thinking it was not good for man to be alone, fashioned woman out of man's side. When God said in Genesis 2 that it was not good for man to be alone, did He mean that Adam was on the planet all by himself? But God had already said to be fruitful and multiply! Or was "Adam" by himself/herself, as two halves of a still-united whole?

Sounds confusing, doesn't it? Much depends on how you view the first two chapters of Genesis. Are they two different accounts of the same creation process, with chapter 1 giving us an overview and chapter 2 giving us more specific detail? Or are they sequential, describing completely different events for us as they unfolded? And if they are sequential, how could it be that God created "Adam" male and female in chapter 1, and then created Eve out of "Adam's" side in chapter 2?

Here are a couple what-if questions for you: What if "Adam" in Genesis 1 was an intersexed being with both male and female organs and attributes? And what if God literally broke "Adam" in half in Genesis 2 when He took the woman out of him/her?

Okay, Kris, I'm done with you and your imagination, you may be thinking right about now. *It's one thing to narrate the creation story from Adam's perspective, but it's another thing to break him in half . . .*

I understand that some people may never have considered the possibilities I bring up in today's reading from the book. And that is what they are—simply possibilities that I am suggesting we take a look at. Take a look yourself and see what *you* think. Could men and women actually be two halves of a whole?

- Today's Scripture reading: Genesis 2; 1 Corinthians 15:42–58
- Today's reading from *Fashioned to Reign*: pages 42–49

Questions to Consider

1. After reading today's *Fashioned to Reign* pages, do you think it possible that "Adam" could have been both male and female before God took woman out of man? Had you ever considered that possibility before?

I don't see it possible

No I haven't.

2. I mention in the book that the Hebrew word *ezer*, translated "helper," is used at least sixteen times in the Old Testament, a few times to describe a wife and all the rest to describe God Himself. What does that do to the concept of a helper being seen as subordinate to the one they help? (See *Fashioned to Reign* pages 45–46.)

That should not happen. Man + woman were made equal.

3. Do you find it significant, as I do, that God uses two completely different words even way back in Genesis to make a clear distinction between having intimacy with someone and having sex? (See *Fashioned to Reign* page 47.) How is it that so many people today manage to confuse the two, or think of them as the same thing? How does this explain some of the troubles in the way men and women view each other?

Because intimate is just having a good loving relationship and also means having sex. The don't see intimacy as 2 meanings, only 1 = sex.

4. Keeping in mind that a wife incubates what her husband cultivates within her, give an example of how a man might become "the victim of his own poisonous garden." (See *Fashioned to Reign* page 49.)

What about giving an example of how he might enjoy good fruits instead?

Be sensitive to what is gestating in the womb

Day 5

Single, yet Whole

I wish that all men were even as I myself. But each one has his own gift from God, one in this manner and another in that.

But I say to the unmarried and to the widows: It is good for them if they remain even as I am.

1 Corinthians 7:7–8 NKJV

If men and women are actually two halves of a whole, what ramifications would that have for singleness? I address that important question more fully in today's book reading. If it takes both men and women to represent God's image to the world, can a single person truly be whole? Can he or she truly be effective in ministry?

The apostle Paul certainly thought so. He felt that singles would do better to remain unencumbered by marriage. He suggested that remaining free of spousal and family concerns, they would also remain freer to pursue ministry. He did not, however, legislate that as a command. He recognized that the ability to remain single permanently is a supernatural gift from God.

There are those to whom God gives a supernatural gift of singleness, and such people can live in wholeness all their lives without marrying. That does not make them half a person! The Holy Spirit supernaturally grafts them into wholeness.

Consider, for example, Mother Teresa, who founded the Missions of Charity known throughout the world. She was also one of the few women ever to receive a Nobel Peace prize. (You will learn more about her in today's reading.) Half a person could never have accomplished half of what she did! She refused to see either her singleness or her womanhood as something that could prevent her from fulfilling her God-given destiny.

We are talking about singleness in today's lesson, but let me mention here as food for thought that although Mother Teresa became the founder and leader of one of the most influential, effective charity organizations in history, she would not have been allowed to become an elder in most of our churches. I must admit, that makes no sense to me. Does it make sense to you?

- Today's Scripture reading: 1 Corinthians 7
- Today's reading from *Fashioned to Reign*: pages 49–53

1. Do you know someone with the supernatural gift of singleness who has chosen to remain that way to pursue ministry? In what ways do you see the Holy Spirit at work in that person to graft him or her into wholeness?

   Yes the love she has for the Lord and she wants to help everybody.

2. Why does it take both feminine and masculine characteristics to represent God to the world? (See *Fashioned to Reign* page 50.)

   It takes both to accurately represent the Godhead.

3. I believe that most male leaders did not resist Mother Teresa's leadership because in caring for the poorest of the poor, she was doing work that most men considered best done by a woman (and a nun) anyway. How will the Church miss out, though, if the mission field is the only place in which Mother Teresas of the future can be empowered?

   The church misses out on the teachings Mother Teresa coved bring to the church.

Session I · Life Application

In one of Day 2's questions, I asked you if you have ever identified so closely with someone in Scripture that you imagined the details of that person's story and the events surrounding his or her life the way I did with Adam. If you have had that experience, take a little time now to journal that Bible personality's story in written form, from his or her perspective. Do your best to stay within the boundaries of Scripture, but do not be afraid to "fill in the blanks" and add some color to your story. If you have already written down such a story, take a few minutes to reread it now.

If you have never done this kind of exercise, think of one of your favorite Bible personalities and reread some Scriptures about him or her now. Then try writing a few paragraphs about an event in that person's life in your own words. Or think about my Adam narrative and write a few paragraphs from Eve's perspective instead.

Your journaling does not have to fill a whole chapter of pages, as my story about Adam did. But I do think you will gain a new perspective into the narratives of Scripture when you become what I call an "imagineer" and give this a try.

Session I · Video Guide

1. When God made Adam, He made him both _____male_____ and _____female_____. And they were made in His _____image_____ and in His _____likeness_____.

2. If you _____oppress_____ women, you lose half the _____revelation_____ of the nature of God.

3. It takes both male and female to _____represent_____ the Godhead.

4. The word *rib* in Scripture actually is the word _____side chamber_____.

5. God took a rib from Adam, and He _____fashioned_____ that rib.

6. God _____formed_____ man (and animals) from dirt, but He _____fashioned_____ woman from more sophisticated material (the rib).

Unmasking
the Devil

Satan wanted to be like God. He wanted to sit in the high places like God. He wanted to rule like God. God thrust him down to a dark and chaotic planet to serve out his death sentence. Then, in the midst of the devil's misery, God remodeled the planet and placed godlike creatures there who could reproduce other godlike creatures, after their kind. . . .

Do you want to know why the devil hates you? Because you were born in the image and likeness of God, whom Lucifer was determined to imitate. We received through creation what the devil was striving for through self-promotion, jealousy and arrogance.

Fashioned to Reign, page 57

Day 1

The Jealous Serpent

You were blameless in your ways
From the day you were created
Until unrighteousness was found in you. . . .
Your heart was lifted up because of your beauty;
You corrupted your wisdom by reason of your splendor.

Ezekiel 28:15, 17

The devil has a demented mind. It took a demented mind—a seriously delusional mind—to think that he could raise himself up to equal the might and majesty of his creator, God. Lucifer already had some God-given might and majesty of his own as a splendorous archangel responsible for leading worship around God's throne. (At least, that is what most theologians infer about him from Scripture.) But all that was not enough. He aspired to claim a share of the glory and worship that belonged to God alone.

The devil's aspirations failed him, and he became the lowest of the low. In fact, so low that after tempting Eve in the Garden, he wound up slithering on his belly on the ground and eating dust as part of God's curse over him. The hostility between the serpent and woman began on that day, and he has hated womankind with a passion ever since.

The devil hates all of humanity for what we represent as children of God, but I believe he hates women even more than he hates men. Having lost his beauty and splendor, I believe the serpent became ugly in the extreme and now seethes with jealousy over the beauty of women. God fashioned women as His gorgeous daughters, and it is more than the serpent can bear to see them worshiping and serving God—as he was meant to do.

- Today's Scripture reading: Isaiah 14:3–17
- Today's reading from *Fashioned to Reign*: pages 55–60

Questions to Consider

1. What does it mean to say that we received through creation what the devil was striving for through self-promotion, jealousy and arrogance? (See *Fashioned to Reign* page 57.) How does that add to his jealousy problem?

   He wanted to be the image of God It makes him hate us.

2. Why do you think we cohabit this planet with the devil? How does our worship of God do damage to the jealous serpent? (See *Fashioned to Reign* page 58).

   So we can do damage to the devil. We praise God so God blesses us n not the devil.

3. Many think that as heaven's worship leader, Lucifer may have used his magnificent musical skills and abilities to draw attention to himself instead of directing worship toward God. What can worship leaders, musicians and singers do to guard their hearts against doing the same?

   Sing Praise to honor God

Day 2

Empowered Eve

Now the serpent was more crafty than any beast of the field which the LORD God had made. And he said to the woman, "Indeed, has God said, 'You shall not eat from any tree of the garden'?"

Genesis 3:1

According to Genesis 3:8, God apparently was in the habit of visiting the Garden in the cool of the day, which left Eve alone with Adam and the animals the rest of the day and night. If Adam was anything like the rest of *man*kind when it comes to making conversation, you can see why Eve might have been delighted to have a talking serpent around to chat with. (Remember, this was before Satan was cursed to crawl on his belly. He still stood upright and could speak Eve's language.)

But I do not think Eve's chattiness was the only reason Satan approached her. I think he knew that Adam and Eve were co-reigning in the Garden, and that Eve in particular was highly persuasive and influential. In a word, Eve was empowered. Neither slave nor servant to Adam, she ruled alongside him and wielded equal authority over the earth. Obviously, Adam was in the habit of listening to her ideas and taking her advice.

Unlike many women today, I do not think Eve had to struggle with male chauvinism or the disempowerment of the fairer sex. She did have one thing in common with many of us, male and female, though. She experienced an identity crisis. When Satan told her that if she ate of the forbidden tree she would "be like God," she found that idea enticing.

Why? Because apparently she had forgotten that she was created in God's image and already *was* like God.

Doesn't that sound like many of us today? It is so easy as believers to forget *who* we are in Christ and concentrate instead on what we *do*—on our performance. We end up performing for our identity rather than operating out of it. That is called *religion*, and it came into the world with Eve's first bite of the forbidden fruit.

- Today's Scripture reading: Genesis 3
- Today's reading from *Fashioned to Reign*: pages 60–62

Questions to Consider
---

1. What evidence from Scripture would lead us to conclude that Eve was not at all a "subservient maid" type, but was both powerful and influential in the Garden? (See *Fashioned to Reign* pages 61–62.)

   She was empowered, persuasive and influential.

2. I mention in today's reading that when it came to eating the forbidden fruit, Adam trusted his wife's insight over God's command. Give an example of how you or someone you know made that same mistake of trusting something or someone else over God. (Actually, the accurate term for it is *sin*.) What is always the result?

   I trusted my husband and joined his Mormon church. Being attacked physically by Satan.

3. Too often, Christians feel they must perform for their identity in Christ rather than simply operating out of it. How did Adam and Eve make that mistake with their God-given identity? (See *Fashioned to Reign* page 62.) Name a few ways in which you and I can avoid that all-too-common error.

   They ate the forbidden fruit, they trusted Satan more than God. Keep focused on God so we never stray

4. The Fall involved more than disobeying God (as if that were not bad enough). It also involved obeying a new master. In what way did Adam and Eve choose a new master in that terrible moment?

   They chose to listen to the Serpent & eat forbidden fruit.

5. How did Adam and Eve's guilt over being naked illustrate that religion has more rules than God has?

God had only 1 Rule.

Day 3

Bruised on the Head

The women who proclaim the good tidings are a great host.

Psalm 68:11

Things happen in the earth and in the demonic realm when women share the Good News. Women empowered to share the Gospel usher in a host of good things in the earth—greater love, greater peace, greater compassion—and along with all those, a greater hatred for anything that has to do with the slithering serpent and his demonic realm.

That last one is part of the curse God put on Satan after the Fall. God declared that there would be enmity, or hostility, between Satan and the woman, and between his seed and her seed, and so it has been. I talk a lot about that in today's reading.

I also talk about how spiritual warfare often focuses on womankind because women are the ones who carry a deep-seated hostility toward the enemy of our souls. Over and over, I have watched as empowered lady believers who are walking out their full destiny in Christ take every opportunity to bruise the enemy and stomp on his head. (Be careful not to get in their way!) The Church cannot afford to lose such a mighty force for ushering in good and routing out evil.

- Today's Scripture reading: Ephesians 6:12; Psalm 51:7; Isaiah 1:16–18
- Today's reading from *Fashioned to Reign*: pages 63–66

1. How was Genesis 3:15, "He shall bruise you on the head, and you shall bruise him on the heel," prophetic in regard to the cross and resurrection? (See *Fashioned to Reign* page 64.)

   He defeated sin on the cross and death, hell and the grave.

2. Throughout history, why has the devil worked overtime to oppress women?

   Woman emulates the Beauty of God more than man. If women empowered, There is new depth of compassion, love, understanding caring & Peace

3. Like many psalms, Psalm 68 has both practical and spiritual applications. What kind of picture do verses 11–14 give us of what happens in the demonic realm when women share the Gospel? (See *Fashioned to Reign* page 66.)

   glad tidings, Women become like a mighty army & drive demonic princes off the mountains.

Day 4

Cursed, yet Redeemed?

Christ redeemed us from the curse of the Law, having become a curse for us—for it is written, "Cursed is everyone who hangs on a tree."

Galatians 3:13

*I*f you are cursed, you can do all the right things but still get the wrong results. If you are redeemed, you can do some wrong things but still be forgiven and blessed. I will take redeemed over cursed anytime! I am so thankful Christ redeemed us from the curse, as the Scripture just above says.

In Genesis 3 God pronounced a curse on Adam, on Eve and on the serpent, but He also promised redemption to humankind through a coming Savior. He delivered on that promise in sending His Son, Jesus Christ.

Think about it. The curse against men was that they would work the ground with great toil, yet it would produce thorns and thistles. After redemption, we are told that what a man sows, he will also reap—a complete reversal of that curse.

When it came to the curse over women, the part about their husbands' ruling over them had the biggest negative impact. Before the curse, Adam and Eve co-reigned; after the curse, husbands dominated wives. And after redemption, husbands still use Scripture to make the case for dominating their wives in the name of the Lord.

No reversal there! If Christ redeemed us from the curse of the Law, why is that still the case? Why are women still under men instead of co-reigning with them? As far as I know, redemption was meant for the whole human race, not just the male half of it.

- Today's Scripture reading: Galatians 3:1–14; Romans 8:1–17
- Today's reading from *Fashioned to Reign*: pages 66–68

Questions to Consider

1. How would you answer the question I pose in today's reading, "What makes us think that men were set free from the curse of the Law at the cross, but that women should still be under the curse that allows husbands to dominate them in the name of God?"

   Jesus released man from the curse on the Cross but it is interpreted as man not mankind being released there women are still under the curse

2. I also mention how significant it was that the soldiers placed a crown of thorns on Jesus' head, symbolizing mankind's redemption from the curse of working the ground, only to have it produce thorns and thistles. What events at the crucifixion/resurrection can you think of that might have symbolized womankind's redemption from the curse of male domination? (Think, for example, about who first was present at the empty tomb and who first saw the risen Lord.)

   The first Jesus saw at the tomb was a woman (mary magdelan) whom was the 1st person to be there on the 3rd day

3. What do you think might need to change in the Church as a result of both men and women receiving the full benefits of our Savior's redemptive acts?

   According to God Christ's Death made us all equal but the men in our church haven't gotten over that men shall have domain over women.

Day 5

Women Warriors

You therefore must endure hardship as a good soldier of Jesus Christ. No one engaged in warfare entangles himself with the affairs of this life, that he may please him who enlisted him as a soldier.

2 Timothy 2:3–4 NKJV

Women warriors are welcome in the Kingdom of God. In spiritual warfare, women warriors are just as dangerous and just as determined as male fighters. We talked in Day 3 about how things really happen in the demonic realm when women share the good news of the Gospel. Every woman believer is enlisted in the army of God as a freedom fighter, fully equipped to bring the light of God's Kingdom into every corner of the earth that is oppressed by the ruler of the dark kingdom.

Not only can women warriors fight for the Kingdom of God; they can lead the way in battle. Think of Joan of Arc. She was a fearless warrior who never doubted her call to lead an army, and not just in the spiritual realm—Joan led in physical battles, too. (I tell you more about her story in today's reading.) As a teenager, she approached the French military and simply announced that she was called to lead their troops. As you can imagine, back in the fifteenth century that was a little hard for the men to take in.

As a young woman, Joan of Arc had no military experience, of course. But she had heard the voice and the call of God, and she let nothing stand in the way of fulfilling her divine destiny. It did not matter that she had to leave the comforts of home for the rigors of battle. It did not matter that some of the French leaders did not respect her. It did not matter that she was shot in the neck with an arrow or thrown in an English dungeon. She kept pressing on toward her goal of heeding the call of God on her life. In doing so, she became instrumental in saving her country from being overtaken by England. Many men had already attempted the same and were failing where she succeeded.

Joan of Arc was one determined woman. Given the time and place of her birth and the society she was born into, I can understand why she had to fight for her right to lead. What I cannot understand is why that fight should still be necessary for women leaders called by God today.

- Today's Scripture reading: Ephesians 6:10–18; Philippians 3:12–16
- Today's reading from *Fashioned to Reign*: pages 69–72

1. Like Joan of Arc, have you ever been absolutely certain that you heard something from God, only to face opposition on every side when you tried to walk it out? What did you do?

   Yes, continued listening to his voice and doing what He was telling me to do or not to do.

2. What might have happened differently in history if Joan of Arc had stayed within her society's stereotypes of what a woman could and could not do?

   France would loose the war, Women would not have the courage strength to face any battle they approched.

3. Following her Savior's example, Joan of Arc paid the ultimate price for stepping up to her divine call, martyrdom. How does her life demonstrate the mark of a true leader?

   Never giving up and when they didn't include her, she didn't give up but carried on.

Session 2 Life Application

In Day 4, question 3, I asked you what you think might need to change in the Church as a result of both men and women receiving the full benefits of our Savior's redemptive acts. Revisit that question now and bring it closer to home. Make a list of three or four areas in your church where there might possibly be inequalities in the way men and women are viewed and treated.

Understand, of course, that I am not asking you to make this list to create division or strife. That would do far more harm than good! So do not take your list and hand it to your church leadership with the demand that something must be done immediately. Rather, take your list and hand it to the Holy Spirit with the request that He show you any part you may have played in fostering those inequalities. Ask Him to show you what you can do personally in your prayer life and in your actions from now on to make sure that everyone, men and women alike, are encouraged to fulfill their God-given destiny.

If there are areas concerning the role of women in your church that you sense you should approach your leadership about, let me advise you to complete this study before you take that step. The remaining sessions will provide you with a solid scriptural foundation to stand on regarding God's calling and gifting of womankind. If you are also part of a *Fashioned to Reign* study group, your discussions may give you some further insight and wisdom about how best to handle such situations.

Session 2 Video Guide

1. The word *enmity* is translated from the Hebrew word for _____.

2. The curse over the _____ is that woman will be _____ toward him.

3. When you think about that curse, it makes sense that almost all _____ _____ is directed at _____.

4. The spear point of spiritual warfare is women. Every religion figures out some way to _____ women. Every culture figures out some way to _____ women.

5. The curse over the woman is that your _____ will rule over you. God did not take _____ and put them over women.

6. Before the curse, Adam and Eve _____.

7. Relationally, Adam needed the _____ to make him _____ because the woman was _____ _____ of the man.

8. Eve was a _____ woman whom the serpent and Adam both _____ to and were both _____ by.

9. Jesus became the curse, and so there is no curse that's _____ or _____ anymore.

10. A curse means you can do the _____ _____, but the _____ _____ still happens. Jesus became a curse so that we could become _____ from the curse.

11. When Jesus died on the cross, He _____ the _____.

12. When God restores, He restores people to a _____ _____ than they began. God doesn't say let Me fix you; He says let Me _____ you (see 2 Corinthians 5:17).

Standing for the Word

For many people, it is hard to understand that not only are there hundreds of contrasting Scriptures in the Bible, but also that much of the Bible is God's documentary on man and not God's commentary on how to live life. When people say, "I live by every word in the Bible," it is not really true. The fact is, there are many words in the Bible you are *not* supposed to live by because God is simply recounting a story and not validating someone's behavior.

Fashioned to Reign, page 84

It is vital that we understand *how* to relate to the Word of God, and it is imperative that we know the difference between God speaking narratively into a situation and God laying out His divine order for our lives. When God speaks narratively, He often gives instructions without correcting the glaringly dysfunctional culture that exists in the circumstances He is narrating. . . . On the other hand, when God gives us commands for life, we must fully embrace them and universally apply them if we want to receive the maximum benefit He intends.

Fashioned to Reign, pages 88–89

Day 1

The Scripture Police

Be diligent to present yourself approved to God, a worker who does not need to be ashamed, rightly dividing the word of truth.

2 Timothy 2:15

I have run into more Scripture Police, those self-appointed members of the "Theological Police Department," than I can count since I started posting on social media such as Facebook. And as I tell you in today's reading from the book, I probably derive far too much pleasure from riling these folks up and sending them off, sirens wailing, in hot pursuit of anyone they believe has committed what they consider a crime against Scripture.

The downside to my fun is that often, *I* am the one they are pursuing. I do it to myself, though, by throwing out some statements I am sure the Scripture Police will want to challenge. Believe me, statements about the empowerment and equality of female believers will do it every time. Putting that topic out there is like pushing the *Hot* button on those with a pharisaical spirit who insist on fulfilling the letter of the law without consulting the Spirit behind it.

As today's Scripture readings tell us, the letter of the law kills, but the Spirit gives life. It is the Spirit who teaches us all things. I wrote in the book, and I will write again here, that *the Word of God without the Spirit of God causes death.* As highly as we respect and revere the Word of God, we cannot apply every word of the Bible *literally* to all situations *universally* without landing ourselves in a lot of hot water.

That seems like a shocking statement, I know. But before you throw away this workbook and my book along with it, allow me to explain. In today's lesson and in this session's other four days, we will take a closer look at the ramifications of trying to apply the Word of God without the Spirit of God. One of the most serious ramifications has been the devaluing and disempowering of women in the Church.

- Today's Scripture reading: 2 Corinthians 3:1–8; John 14:16–26
- Today's reading from *Fashioned to Reign*: pages 73–80

1. Have you ever considered that there is a difference between *believing* every word of the Bible and *living* every word of the Bible? Many believers think the two concepts are synonymous, but why is that *not* the case? (We will talk much more about this in the days just ahead.)

   Some things God says in the Bible He wants you to do, other things He's saying are just examples or something. events

2. If you make use of social media, undoubtedly you have noticed that theological debates on sites like Facebook can become quite heated (especially if the Scripture Police get involved). What kind of theological debates have you posted comments about? Do you feel the exchanges were beneficial to the participants? Why or why not?

   Debates about Walmart. Not all Participant Because some of them just don't want to hear the truth and won't believe it.

3. Have you ever had an experience like mine and Kathy's in the airport, where the letter of the law and the spirit of the law clashed? Isn't it frustrating? What did you do? (Hopefully you handled yourself with more grace in the situation than I did!)

4. Many Christians with a religious spirit view the concepts of "situational relevance" and "contextual application" as dangerous and degrading when applied to the Word of God. How do you view those concepts? Can they be dangerous? Can they be helpful? (We

will talk much more about these things as we go through the rest of this session.)

_____

_____

_____

Day 2

Truth or Travesty?

Knowledge is easy to one who has understanding.

Proverbs 14:6

We ended Day 1 by talking a little about the concept of applying the Bible literally to every situation universally. I give examples in today's reading of the seeming contradictions such a practice can emphasize between different Scriptures. Of course, we know that the truths of the Bible never contradict each other, although that may be our perception due to misunderstanding. There are, however, hundreds of contrasting Scriptures that get in the way of a literal application of the Bible's every word to every situation. (You will see what I mean as you read today's pages.)

When it comes to applying the Word of God to our everyday lives, the fact is that there are a whole lot of words in Scripture we are *not* supposed to live out! How can I say such a thing? Because God gives us both documentary and commentary in His Word. Documentary is His narrative about what Bible characters did, often without any sense that He condones their actions. (In many cases, just the opposite is true.) Commentary contains His instruction on how we are to live our lives.

I will return to that idea again in the remaining days of this session, but you can start to see the picture. While we admire Esther for her courage and loyalty to her people in the pages of Scripture, we would never apply the narrative about her to our daughters' lives by suggesting that they sleep with some big company CEO so that they could gain godly influence in a larger corporation. Applying the Bible in that way would make no sense whatsoever. In fact, it would be a travesty far removed from the truth of what God intends for His precious daughters.

If people really insisted on applying every word of the Bible literally, they could wind up committing one travesty after another, which is exactly what has happened when it comes to the disempowerment of women in the Church. I believe Scripture clearly shows that it was never God's heart for the female half of His children to be devalued and dominated. We have to understand God's heart in order to understand how to apply our knowledge of Scripture in ways that fulfill His purposes.

- Today's Scripture reading: Esther chapters 1 and 2; Genesis 20
- Today's reading from *Fashioned to Reign*: pages 80–85

1. When I say there is "truth held in tension" between different Scriptures, what do you think I mean? (See my examples on pages 80–82 of *Fashioned to Reign*.)

   That we do honor our Parents.

2. How do we resolve some of this "truth held in tension" between contrasting Scriptures? (See *Fashioned to Reign* page 83.)

   We must have a Relationship with God. You still need the Holy Spirit to get the Revelation

3. How does my example of the sign on the studio door, *Stop Nursing Mothers Only*, help you understand how people can read signs in Scripture through what I call the lens of restrictions? (See *Fashioned to Reign* pages 83–84.)

   If you look thru the lens of restrictions you see women not equal.

4. Suggest some ways in which people who devalue women may have mixed up documentary or narrative with commentary when it comes to their application of the Scriptures.

   Women can easily be deceived

Day 3

At the Core

So take care *how* you listen . . .
Luke 8:18, emphasis added

Core values are the principles, standards and virtues at the center of the way we live, love and think. Think about the values at the core of King Solomon's writings. Gifted by God with wisdom itself, Solomon was the wisest man who ever lived. He shared his wisdom with us in his greatest contribution to humanity, the book of Proverbs. Throughout Proverbs, Solomon expressed his core values, giving us a glimpse into all the insight he held in his heart.

Then some time went by and some things changed, and Solomon took up his pen again and gave us another book, Ecclesiastes. The problem is, much of what is at the core of Ecclesiastes completely differs from what is at the core of Proverbs. In the Scriptures we look at in today's reading, you will see just what I mean.

What happened? In a word, *relationship*—or lack thereof. As Solomon became older and pursued false idols, his relationship with God changed. When he became confused and depressed as a result, his core values became flawed, and he out-and-out contradicted some of the pearls of great wisdom he had penned for us in Proverbs. That necessitates some discernment on our part about *how* we listen to Solomon's words and what we see in them. Some of them are words of life that we are meant to follow; some of them are words of death that we are meant to avoid following.

How do we discern the difference? In a word, *relationship*—our relationship to God. As we approach the contrasting and even contradictory parts of Scripture such as Proverbs and Ecclesiastes, our relationship with God needs to be at the core of our approach. We need to know His heart and be guided by His Holy Spirit. Or to put it another way, we need to have our "Son-glasses" on, which provide powerful protection against the distortion of Scripture. (More about that in today's reading.) Seeing everything in Scripture through the lens of our Savior's cross and resurrection will keep us solid at the core.

- Today's Scripture reading: Luke 8:4–21
- Today's reading from *Fashioned to Reign*: pages 86–92

Questions to Consider

1. What is the difference between contrasting verses and contradicting verses in Scripture? What examples does Ecclesiastes give us of contradicting verses? (See *Fashioned to Reign* page 88.)

   Contrast is looking at 2 different sides must be both true and in certain context.

2. How did the question of slavery in the American Civil War illustrate the deadly ramifications of confusing God's narratives in Scripture with God's commands? (See *Fashioned to Reign* page 89.) Can you see how the question of empowering women in the Church today might be the result of similar confusion?

   Scripture say Masters Grant your slaves justice in fairness.
   Eve was deceived by satan & shouldn't be in leadership.

3. How do you think people's core values predispose them to see and hear things in a certain way? When those core values are flawed, what happens to a person's ability to correctly understand Scripture?

   Their core values are flawed.

4. Why is it so important to view the Scriptures through the "Songlasses" of Calvary's cross, both in general and particularly when it comes to God's divine purposes for women? (See *Fashioned to Reign* page 91.)

   To see the value in women to make them equal to man.

Day 4

A New Operating System

But now faith, hope, love, abide these three; but the greatest
of these is love.

1 Corinthians 13:13

Computer techies can tell you more than I can about why, from time
to time, new operating systems come out for your computer. But
this much I know: There is a huge difference between reading about
a new operating system (OS) that is hitting the market and experiencing
it yourself by actually using it. Reading all the specs about a new OS on
paper (or onscreen) can be a bit of a flat experience, (unless you are a
techie who enjoys that sort of reading), whereas interacting with a new
OS and immersing yourself in it for the first time can open up a whole
new world.

I describe for you in today's reading a dream I had some years ago in
which God told me He was releasing "a new operating system" on His
people. It was one thing to dream about it, and I describe that for you
in the book. It has been a whole different thing in the time since then to
live it out and interact with it. For me, concepts like *courage* and *peace*
and *power* and *truth* and *love* have turned from words on a page into
multidimensional, interactive experiences with new revelation. Christi-
anity is, after all, meant to be an interactive faith, not a "read about it"
system of philosophy. That is why God also told me in that dream that
the stagnant mind-sets of religious structures must give way to a living
organism that is the Church.

Another thing God showed me in that dream was that there are levels
of truth inherent in His Word. Some truths are greater, or weightier, than

others. When we fail to take that into account, we can misapply Scripture and create environments that destroy people rather than building them up. (See my examples in the book.)

The devil likes to use Scripture to destroy people. He twists it and tempts us to misapply it until all we have left is *religion*, not a relationship with the living God and a life lived out in His operating system. Religion oppresses people and puts them in bondage. Religion oppresses *women* and puts them in bondage. And we are not just talking the "Christian religion" here. Take a look at what some of the other religions of the world demand of women. God's operating system, on the other hand, rescues His daughters and restores them to their rightful place alongside His sons.

- Today's Scripture reading: Luke 5:36–39; Genesis 9:20–27
- Today's reading from *Fashioned to Reign*: pages 92–96

1. Is there a word (or words) God has revealed to you by experience rather than by simple definition, the way He did with me in my dream? How did that change your understanding of the word?

   We do not understand the truth out of order out of context + out of proper timing (This is Perversion)

2. What do you think I mean by suggesting that not all truth is created equal? How does our grasp of that affect the way we deal with people? (See *Fashioned to Reign* pages 93–94.)

   Hope - faith - love - the Greatest is love
   Talk to them with love + not judge

3. In today's reading, I make the statement that the Word of God in the hands of anyone besides the Holy Spirit always leads to religion, bondage and death. Give an example or two of situations you have run across that confirm the truth of that statement.

Day 5

Out from Under

It was for freedom that Christ set us free; therefore keep standing firm and do not be subject again to a yoke of slavery.

Galatians 5:1

*H*arriet Tubman was a third-generation slave. She was born in slavery and raised in slavery, yet she did not stay in slavery. She fought her way out from under that curse, journeying to freedom and taking countless others with her. I retell her story briefly in today's reading because I like her kind of determination and outrageous courage.

You probably already know that Harriet was called the Moses of her people and that she traveled on the Underground Railroad to lead them to freedom. Did you know that she also served as a Civil War cook, nurse, armed scout and spy? She even became the first woman to lead an armed mission in the Civil War! Beyond the war, she became a leader in the fight for women's rights (no surprise there). She traveled all across the country as a keynote speaker in the suffragist movement. Hers is an amazing, almost unbelievable story.

What empowered and encouraged Harriet, an illiterate slave woman who was "powerless" against her oppressors, to accomplish so much? Certainly her passionate longing for freedom drove her, but she had a deeper passion than that, and a greater power available to her. Harriet was deeply devoted to her Lord and Savior. She believed that God was good and just. She believed that He had called her to set the captives free. She trusted Him to give her the wisdom and protection necessary to fulfill that divine destiny. And He did.

Like Harriet, you and I were born into slavery. And the prince of this fallen world we live in, the devil, wants every human being to stay in slavery. But we, too, have more available to us than meets the eye. We, too, have a Savior who is good and just, who has called us to find freedom in Him and to set the captives free. That call out from under the curse is for all of us, male and female alike.

- Today's Scripture reading: Galatians 5:13–25
- Today's reading from *Fashioned to Reign*: pages 97–100

Questions to Consider

1. Harriet Tubman's identity was in God and His purposes for her, not in the circumstances of her birth, captivity or gender. How does knowing who you are in Christ make a difference in what you can accomplish for the Kingdom?

   Knowing who you are in Christ makes use confident and know everything is possible thru Jesus Christ.

2. Even as an illiterate, third-generation slave woman, what did Harriet understand about the empowerment of women that many people today still do not comprehend?

   They have power

3. Have you ever felt as though you face overwhelming odds in one battle after another in your Christian walk? Notice that Harriet's fighting spirit did not diminish after she won her freedom and the evil of slavery was abolished. She marched onto a new battlefield, women's rights, and kept fighting for freedom there. What can we learn from her example as we face our own spiritual battles?

   As long as you know yourself in Christ you can do anything. To not be afraid because you can do it.

Session 3 Life Application

I talked a lot in this session about the truth held in tension between different Scriptures and about how the letter of the law kills, but the Spirit brings life. I cannot overemphasize enough how a literal application of the Scriptures universally to all situations has resulted in a staggering amount of bondage and oppression both in the Church and in society at large (think about my example of slavery in Civil War times). I also cannot overemphasize enough that the guidance of the Holy Spirit in applying and living out the Word of God brings freedom and truth.

Ask the Lord right now to help you learn even better to process the Word of God through the lens of the Holy Spirit. Ask for insight into any areas where you may have been trying to apply Scriptures literally that were never intended for universal application. Be honest with yourself, and take a careful look at your motivation. Was it more important to you to walk in truth and love in those areas, or more important to be "right"?

Also ask the Lord if He would consider you a badge-carrying member of the Scripture Police in any area, and be prepared to turn in your badge if He brings any areas to mind. This can be a difficult step to take, especially if you have tended to be militant about the "submissive" role of women in the Church. But if you will voluntarily turn in your badge in any areas where you have joined the Scripture Police, I think you will find that the promotion of the Lord that can come your way will far exceed any satisfaction you got from being on that spiritual hot button squad.

Session 3 Video Guide

1. The ___letter___ kills, but the ___Spirit___ gives life (see 2 Corinthians 3:6).

2. The Word of God in the hands of the ___devil___ is not ___true___.

3. It takes the Word of God and the ___Spirit___ to make truth.

4. Proverbs shows what happens when the ___wisest___ man in the world has a ___relationship___ with God. Ecclesiastes shows what happens when the ___wisest___ man in the world ___looses___ relationship with God.

5. The ___appreciation___ of the Word of God needs to be ___directed___ by the Holy Spirit.

6. The Spirit of God ___leads___ us into all ___truth___.

7. You ___process___ the Bible through the ___lens___ of the Holy Spirit.

8. Truth is held in ___tension___.

9. Some of the Bible is a ___documentary___, and some of the Bible is a ___commentary___. Sometimes God is telling us a ___story___; other times, God is saying, "This is how it should happen."

10. Millions and millions of Christian women have been ___oppressed___ because people have taken a documentary and they've ___made___ it a commentary.

The First Women's Lib Movement

I have to admit that before I wrote this book, I never understood the radical message of gender equality that the gospel writers were trying to convey through the life of Jesus. Yes, I knew that Jesus hated religion. I was aware that He was a countercultural radical who overturned the deceptive tables of hypocrisy and drove the moneychangers out of the Temple. Having read the Bible every day for thirty-plus years, I understood that quite a few women hung around Jesus. Yet because I did not have a real grasp on the oppressive culture of first-century Judaism and the massive mistreatment of women during the days of Christ, I totally missed one of the most profound messages of the gospels—that Jesus championed the equality of women.

Fashioned to Reign, page 110

Day 1

Jesus' Many Girlfriends

Why do you bother the woman? For she has done a good deed to Me. . . . Truly I say to you, wherever this gospel is preached in the whole world, what this woman has done will also be spoken of in memory of her.

Matthew 26:10, 13

In first-century Judaism, men were barely on speaking terms with women. Men considered women—even wives and daughters—as little more than property, and expendable property at that. The position of Jewish women at the time was much like what we saw in Afghanistan in our time, before the American invasion. An Israelite woman of the first century had no vote, no voice and no influence. She also had very little involvement with the Temple or the Torah. For the most part, women were relegated to the "outer courts" of every area of life.

Then came Jesus. He brought women into His inner circle, and that turned His world upside down all by itself. Women, who were not allowed to speak to an unrelated man in public, traveled with Him. Women, who were not allowed to be taught the Torah, called him Teacher. In His conversation with Martha about her brother, Lazarus, Jesus even released to a woman the deepest revelation of God's resurrection power.

What was He thinking? That was the question on the mind of almost every man who was Jesus' contemporary. And sometimes I think that more than a few Christian men today are still asking it! The men of His time could not understand why Jesus had so many friends who were girls. (Which is what I meant by "Jesus' many girlfriends." Obviously, He had no romantic or intimate relationships.) The gospels are full of

His interactions with women, and every interaction showed how much He valued and respected them. We men of today would do much better, as would the Church, if we would follow His example.

- Today's Scripture reading: Acts 16:14–15; John 11:1–46; Matthew 26:6–13
- Today's reading from *Fashioned to Reign*: pages 101–108

1. In what ways do you see that the Church has tried to domesticate the Lion of the tribe of Judah? (See *Fashioned to Reign* page 101.)

_____

_____

_____

2. I related in today's reading that in almost all first-century Gentile cultures, women and men were co-equals in leading religious worship, yet in first-century Judaism, women were barred from being much more than onlookers in the outer court of the synagogues. What is wrong with that picture when it comes to the daughters of God's chosen people?

The men considered women were
Relegated to the outer courts n They had
no vote, no voice & no influence.

3. While we know that Jesus loves us all, the Bible only specifically mentions four names of people whom Jesus loved during His time on earth, and two of the names were of women. (See *Fashioned to Reign* page 105.) How might that be significant?

Mary n Martha   He showed He
didn't consider them lesser than men.

4. Scripture records a number of interactions Jesus had with Mary and Martha, who were two of His closest friends. What do those interactions show about the way Jesus related to women? Beyond that, what do they show about the way He related to different personality

They weren't Taboo.
Everybody was welcome to sit and
talk n learn with Jesus

types? (See *Fashioned to Reign* pages 104–108 for my discussion of some of those interactions.)

_____

_____

_____

Day 2

Questionable Company

From that city many of the Samaritans believed in Him because of the word of the woman who testified . . .

John 4:39

*J*esus did more than teach women and hang out with them. He hung out with women of ill repute. The company He kept was not always of the highest caliber in the eyes of the religious leaders. In their opinion, Jesus hung out with some downright questionable company—a prostitute who wet His feet with her tears and wiped them with her hair; Mary Magdalene, who had been possessed of seven demons; the woman at the well who had had five husbands plus a live-in and was a Samaritan on top of it. Yet in every case, Jesus saw something in the woman that was valuable, a feminine treasure.

I love the question Jesus put to Simon the Pharisee when a prostitute interrupted their dinner to wash Jesus' feet: "Do you *see* this woman?" *See* as in *acknowledge her, look at her, recognize her as a person.* We talked in Day 1 of this session about how the men of His time were not at all in the habit of doing so with women. Jesus, on the other hand, recognized the personhood of every woman He came across. He treated each one as His Father's precious daughter.

Did you realize that the first time Jesus revealed Himself as the Messiah—the first time He actually said those words to someone—it was to the Samaritan woman at the well? That was paradigm-shattering on so many levels. And as soon as she got the revelation, she ran back to her village to spread the word, becoming the world's first evangelist. I guarantee that she would never have qualified as an elder in any of our churches, yet Jesus *saw* her for who she could become in Him. Again, we men and the Church as a whole would do better if we would follow His example.

- Today's Scripture reading: John 4:1–30; 8:1–11
- Today's reading from *Fashioned to Reign*: pages 108–115

1. Why is it all too easy to look *through* people we do not consider worthy of our notice rather than *seeing* them for who they could become in Christ? How can we correct that?

   People go by 1st impression and Judge on what they see or hear about the person. Get to know them, to listen to them.

2. Why does having some grasp on the culture of first-century Judaism help us understand the gospels and Jesus' actions in them more fully?

   They devalued women then. Jesus Regarded them all the same and knew what they could do and be.

3. How does being familiar with the situation women faced in the first century help us understand Jesus' interactions with them?

4. True leaders are acknowledged by titles, not created by them. What does that mean to you? (See *Fashioned to Reign* pages 114–115.)

   You could have a Title and a plaque on your desk but no one follows you. A True leader has people who listen to them and follow.

Day 3

A Mother's Influence

When the wine ran out, the mother of Jesus said to Him, "They have no wine." And Jesus said to her, "Woman, what does that have to do with us? My hour has not yet come." His mother said to the servants, "Whatever He says to you, do it."

John 2:3–5

You are probably familiar with the story of the wedding at Cana. The host ran out of wine, an embarrassing faux pas. Mary comes to her son and says the wine is gone. Jesus tells her He is in no position to do anything about it because His time has not yet come (for public miracles), and then He goes and does exactly what Mom tells Him to do.

What a mark of respect for His mother. Jesus was thirty at the time and had already picked His disciples, who were present there with Him. In front of friends, family and those he would lead, Jesus acquiesced to His mother's request.

You cannot tell me Mary had no influence with the Son of God, who was also her son. But I think perhaps her influence went further with Him than we realize. As we talked about in Day 2 of this session, Jesus' ministry often extended to women of ill repute. I think it quite possible that He first learned to extend such women grace through the example of His mother.

After all, Mary had once been a woman of ill repute. When she became pregnant with the Son of God by the power of the Holy Spirit, I do not imagine that story sat so well with those around her. Even Joseph, her fiancé, did not buy into such a theory and planned to divorce her quietly.

It took an angel to convince him of the truth, and I am sure not everyone she knew was the recipient of an angelic appearance that detailed her condition for them. So it only follows that having been in difficult circumstances herself, Mary would feel compassion for others of her sex who found themselves in less-than-perfect situations.

Jesus followed Mary's example. In today's reading from the book, you will see how Jesus often laid the responsibility for sexual immorality on men, whereas the whole of the Old Testament tended to lay the blame on women. What a reversal! I am sure His mother, at least, was pleased.

- Today's Scripture reading: John 2:1–11; 5:19–24; Matthew 5:27–32
- Today's reading from *Fashioned to Reign*: pages 115–122

Questions to Consider

1. Why do you suppose Jesus chose to submit to His mother's request, against His initial judgment, at the wedding at Cana?

   The Respect he had for his mother

2. Although all of Jesus' teachings about immorality should apply equally to both men and women, why do you suppose He chose to direct His warnings toward men, in a polar-opposite reversal of the typical Old Testament stance?

   They had the choice to be with them or not and chose to be with them.

3. Jesus shocked even His disciples with His stance against divorce. They reacted by saying then it is better not to marry. How do you suppose the women of His day reacted to Jesus' teachings about marriage and divorce?

Day 4

Making Women Welcome

But the woman fearing and trembling, aware of what had happened to her, came and fell down before Him and told Him the whole truth. And He said to her, "Daughter, your faith has made you well; go in peace and be healed of your affliction."

Mark 5:33–34

*T*he incident of the woman with the issue of blood was no issue for Jesus. (You will read her story in one of today's Scripture readings.) Yes, Jewish law quarantined any woman on her menstrual cycle and declared that anyone who came in contact with her was unclean. Jesus looked at the woman who touched the hem of His garment differently. Rather than her making *Him* unclean with her touch, He made *her* clean. I think Jesus used the incident to show the crowd that women were welcome in His presence in any condition, menstrual cycle or no.

Contrary to first-century Jewish culture, Jesus welcomed women into His presence continually (and He still does). I have already mentioned that many among the disciples who traveled with Him were women. The Greek word used in Luke's gospel for the women who contributed to Jesus' support is *diakoneo*, the same word used in Acts for the men appointed as deacons to serve tables. The fact that the gospel writers mentioned women at all, especially in any position of significance, was a radical departure from the social and religious norms of their day. Jesus made it His business to cause radical departures from the norm.

Although it is true that not one book of the Bible is attributed to a woman author, it is also true that the words and stories of women are recorded throughout Scripture. To discount or discredit feminine contributions to the Word of God would rob us of a great deal of important teaching. To discount or discredit feminine contributions to the Church today would likewise rob us. We need to make women as welcome today as Jesus did.

- Today's Scripture reading: Mark 5:25–34; Luke 15
- Today's reading from *Fashioned to Reign*: pages 122–128

Questions to Consider

1. In today's reading, I talk about the three parables Jesus told in Luke 15 in which a character in the story represented God. What do you think the reaction of the scribes and Pharisees might have been to the story in which Jesus used a woman looking for a lost coin to represent God?

   _____

   _____

   _____

2. In its oppression of the feminine, how does religion rob people of seeing the full spectrum of the nature of God? (See *Fashioned to Reign* pages 124–125.)

   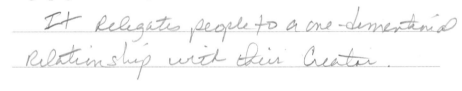
   It Relegates people to a one-dimentional Relationship with their Creator.

   _____

3. Jesus chose not to promote any of His female disciples into the position of one of His twelve apostles. Does my explanation of why He did that make sense to you? (See *Fashioned to Reign* page 125.) Do you think He would still need to make the same choice today?

   Yes I do.

   _____

   _____

Day 5

How Embarrassing!

Therefore take up the whole armor of God, that you may be able to withstand in the evil day, and having done all, to stand.

Ephesians 6:13 NKJV

I have said it more than once in my book, and I will say it again here: I cannot get around how embarrassing it is that women in the world are more empowered than women in the Church. Shouldn't it be the other way around? Shouldn't our sisters in the Church be among the most powerful, influential, mobilized force for good on the planet?

The women who walked with Jesus were world shakers and paradigm breakers—just look at their roles surrounding the crucifixion and resurrection. How can we relegate women in the Church today to anything less? Yet in many churches today, a woman who is the CEO of a large corporation or the mother of several children walks in only to find herself relegated to a subservient role. She can be anything her heart desires out in society, but she cannot talk, teach or help lead in the Church. Do you see anything wrong with that picture? I do.

Like the women at Jesus' cross and tomb who refused to hide away with the men while there was something more to be done, the woman I talk about at the end of today's reading had to stand up and take action in a difficult situation. Or more precisely, Rosa Parks stayed seated and took action. While many others faced the same situation and did nothing, Rosa Parks in one courageous act became the Mother of Civil Rights. Her decision to face prejudice head-on one day as she rode home on a bus after work triggered a series of events that changed America as we knew it. She went from victim to victor, and she led others to victory over evil. In a spiritual sense, our churches are full of women who are equipped to do the same.

- Today's Scripture reading: Galatians 3:26–29
- Today's reading from *Fashioned to Reign*: pages 128–132

Questions to Consider

1. Do you think it is true in some cases to say that the Church is just another men's club that reduces women? In what areas might this be true?

2. How do you think things might be different for women if Jesus actually had the opportunity to lead in some of His churches today?

3. Why do you suppose that Rosa Parks's individual and somewhat isolated act so highly motivated male leaders among her people to stand with her and take action? Could it have had anything to do with her being a woman?

Session 4 Life Application

I asked in one of this session's discussion questions what would be different today if Jesus actually came back in the flesh right now and had an opportunity to lead some of today's churches. Take a few minutes to think about this on a personal level. Ask the Holy Spirit to show you what might be different in your home and in your church if Jesus were here to actually take the lead. What might it look like on a practical level if Jesus were leading the way, especially in regard to the role and treatment of women?

Now ask the Holy Spirit what you can do—not your pastor or ministry leader or spouse—what *you* can do in your position or role to usher in the Kingdom of God here on earth by doing things the way Jesus would do them. What needs to change in your heart and attitudes to bring God's Kingdom to earth?

If you are a man, what needs to change about the way you value women and their contributions? If you are a woman, what needs to change about the way you value yourself and other women?

These are not easy questions, but with the Holy Spirit's guidance and the solid foundation of Scripture, you can construct a better paradigm than you had before regarding the role of women in the church and in society. As I said at the start, it's time to incite a revolution!

Session 4 Video Guide

1. The Judaizers claimed _____ as their father, but they actually added _____ times as many laws as Moses actually gave them from God. Almost _____ of those new laws were against women.

2. The curse put _____ under _____. It did not put _____ over _____.

3. The most famous scribe of Jesus' day said, "I'd rather _____ the Torah than _____ it to a woman."

4. It wasn't just countercultural, it was _____ for Jesus to be teaching Mary (women).

5. Jesus had come to set the oppressed _____, and there was nobody more oppressed in the days of Christ than _____.

6. Because women were eliminated from all _____, therefore the _____ side of God was completely gone.

7. _____ was women's work; men did not _____. But Jesus weeps because He is saying to Mary and to women everywhere, "I get you. I connect with you. I _____ you."

8. The world is so absent of the _____, _____, _____ side of God because we have left women out of our culture and oppressed them.

Just a Misunderstanding

The problem is that oftentimes, the context of an epistle is either misunderstood or ignored, and then well-meaning people take God's situational counsel and try to enforce it universally. You would think people would realize that when they are applying Scripture in a way that is unredemptive, disempowering, oppressive or dishonoring, it somehow violates the nature of God. Yet people continue to make such applications, while ignoring the *full* counsel of the Word of God and undermining the purpose of the cross of Christ.

Ignoring the contextual settings of Scripture and applying the epistles universally has resulted in unimaginable consequences such as slavery and a preposterous gender prejudice toward women. For centuries, women were forced to take vows of silence when entering a church building and were reduced to being powerless citizens of the Kingdom. For too long, women have lived in a two-class environment most often promoted, perpetuated and propelled by misinformed believers.

Fashioned to Reign, page 138

Day 1

Silence, Woman!

The women are to keep silent in the churches; for they are not permitted to speak, but are to subject themselves, just as the Law also says. If they desire to learn anything, let them ask their own husbands at home; for it is improper for a woman to speak in church.

1 Corinthians 14:34–35

Do I acknowledge that the above verses are part of Scripture? Absolutely. Do I agree that they are part of the inerrant Word of God? Positively. Do I therefore conclude that all women everywhere should keep silent whenever they walk through the doors of a church? Absolutely, positively *NOT*.

How can I say that? Stick with me through the five days of this session and find out. For a long time I did my best to ignore such verses or rationalize them away, but in time that was not enough. Looking at my wife, daughters and granddaughters and realizing what they would face if Scripture were misapplied, I realized I had to search out the truth for the sake of the women I love. I trust that whether male or female, you will do the same during the course of this *Fashioned to Reign* study.

The apostle Paul penned the verses in question, along with some other verses that continue to plague us about this topic of women in the Church. From Paul comes most of our understanding about the restrictions we supposedly should place on women believers. But I believe that rather than catching Paul's meaning and getting it right, we have gone further down the path of misunderstanding him.

How can I say that? I base my statement on the full counsel of the Word of God. Of the forty authors writing the Bible over a period of 1,450 years in several countries, only Paul seemed to restrict women in any way from teaching or leading. And of the nine different locations or people Paul wrote to, he only seemed to set restrictions on women in three locations. The question then becomes, why would Paul have empowered women equally alongside men in some places and limited women in others? Perhaps he never intended for God's situational counsel to be applied literally and universally to all contexts ever afterward. Perhaps God never intended it, either. Let's take a closer look at that possibility in the days just ahead.

- Today's Scripture reading: 1 Corinthians 14:26–40; Luke 10:25–28
- Today's reading from *Fashioned to Reign*: pages 133–138

Questions to Consider

1. Like me, have you ever tended to ignore or rationalize away difficult verses of Scripture about women and their place in the Church? Why doesn't that work? Why can it be dangerous?

2. Had you ever considered before now that first-century churches did not have the opportunity to apply all of the epistles to every situation universally? Why was that the case? (See *Fashioned to Reign* page 137.)

3. Unless they were one of the specific locations involved, would most of the New Testament churches even have known about Paul's restrictions on women in certain places? What implications does that have for us today?

4. What is the difference in application between the Pentateuch and the epistles? In other words, why can't a New Testament Christian relate to the epistles in the same way as an Old Testament Jew related to the book of the Law? (See *Fashioned to Reign* pages 137–138.)

5. Throughout Church history, taking Scriptures out of context has always resulted in misunderstandings and misapplications. Can you think of a couple key areas besides the role of women in which this practice has caused ongoing issues?

_____

_____

_____

Day 2

Journey Back in Time

For how do you know, O wife, whether you will save your husband? Or how do you know, O husband, whether you will save your wife?

1 Corinthians 7:16

*I*n today's reading, I suggest three possible responses you may be having to *Fashioned to Reign* and this accompanying workbook: (1) You are angry and are busily forming counterarguments in your mind. (2) You are open-minded but are secretly hoping Paul's restrictions on women will stand. (3) You are already convinced that the Gospel empowers women and are thrilled to place your conviction on some solid footing.

Whichever category you fall into, be patient enough to journey back in time with me in today's lesson to the three geographic locations Paul specifically addressed concerning women. I have a feeling that when we see what was going on in those places, it will shed some light on this important topic we are considering together.

All three of the cities that received a letter from Paul containing some seeming restrictions on women—Corinth, Ephesus and the island of Crete—worshiped female deities. That was their main commonality, which is highly significant (you can read more about each city in today's book pages). The men in this new Christian faith were struggling to understand how to treat sisters in Christ who were saved out of an immoral, pagan religious environment in which women played a dominant role in worship. Paul wrote 1 Corinthians in response to questions the Corinthians had already asked him in a previous letter, and it is important to note that he addressed his responses not to men about women, but to a congregation of both men and women. That is also significant.

Along with his seemingly restrictive verses, Paul wrote that wives have authority over their husbands' bodies, and that an unbelieving wife can sanctify an unbelieving husband—and those are just for starters. For a first-century Jewish male and a former Pharisee no less, Paul expresses some astonishing and radical ideas about women and their place in the Church. In light of that, it makes no sense to pull a few seemingly restrictive verses out of context and apply them literally and universally, without considering the full import of everything else Paul had to say.

- Today's Scripture reading: Acts 27:1–13; Ephesians 2:1–3
- Today's reading from *Fashioned to Reign*: pages 138–145

─── *Questions to Consider* ─────────────────────

1. Which of the three responses I mention are you having to *Fashioned to Reign*? Ask yourself if you have fallen into one of those categories based on the teachings or opinions of others. Rather than "falling into" a mind-set about women based on someone else's say-so, don't you agree that it would be better to stay with this study and explore for yourself the evidence it presents for the empowerment of female believers?

_____

_____

_____

2. What effects do you think it might have had on a young, first-century Church to be planted within a culture that embraces female deities and is used to women dominating religious practices and worship? How might that situation create some confusion about gender roles and relationships in a newly formed congregation of believers?

_____

_____

_____

3. From 1 Corinthians 7:1, "Now concerning the things about which you wrote," and from other verses throughout the epistle, what appears to be the context of Paul's letter? Why does this introduce somewhat of a challenge to our understanding of Paul's comments? (See *Fashioned to Reign* page 142.)

_____

_____

_____

4. As I ask on page 144 of the book, does a person's sex trump a relationship with God when it comes to leadership and authority? What is your current answer to that question based on? (We will

keep examining different aspects of this question and search for biblically solid answers in the days ahead.)

_____

_____

_____

Day 3

It Depends on Who You Are

But I want you to understand that Christ is the head of every *aner* [Greek], and the *aner* is the head of a *gune* [Greek], and God is the head of Christ.

1 Corinthians 11:3 (author version)

*I*n 1 Corinthians, Paul laid out a governmental strategy for empowering women to minister. Just how empowered you think women are, however, depends on who you are. The core values you hold about the relationship between men and women give rise to how you will view Paul's instructions.

But shouldn't our understanding of Scripture be black-and-white? After all, Scripture is Scripture, right? Why do all these gray areas keep popping up? Why all this debate about what, exactly, Paul meant? The kicker is that the Greek word for man, *aner*, is identical to the Greek word for husband, and the Greek word for woman, *gune*, is identical to the Greek word for wife. So if you are a scholar who believes the husband should be the head of the wife, you translate the above verse to reflect that stance. If you are a scholar who believes *all* men should be the head of *all* women, you translate it in an entirely different way.

You can see the complications that arise in translating this one, single verse about men and women in such widely different ways, and I talk more extensively about that in today's reading. Just the various ways in which our more familiar translations of the Bible render that verse will make your head spin! Which translation you subscribe to totally changes for you the scope of influence men and women have with each other.

What to do? That also depends on who you are. If you are someone whose mind is made up to keep all women subjugated to all men in the Church, you are not going to look any more closely at this than your favorite English translation. If you are someone who wants the whole counsel of God, there is much more to consider. No matter who you are, though, one thing from Scripture is clear: Headship and authority were never meant to be used as a means of reducing or oppressing someone else. Consider these words of Jesus: "On the contrary, he who is greatest among you, let him be as the younger, and he who governs as he who serves" (Luke 22:26 NKJV).

- Today's Scripture reading: Luke 22:24–27
- Today's reading from *Fashioned to Reign*: pages 145–152

—— *Questions to Consider* ——————————

1. I mention in today's pages from the book that there were a lot of bald-headed women in Corinth, which prompted Paul to make those comments in 1 Corinthians 11 about women and their head coverings. In Corinth, what did having a shaved head symbolize about a woman? What did a covering of long hair reflect? (See *Fashioned to Reign* page 146.) Is that symbolism contextual or still accurate today?

_____

_____

_____

2. How does the Bible version you most often use translate *aner* and *gune* in 1 Corinthians 11:3? How might that have shaped your conclusions about how men and women in the Church relate to one another?

_____

_____

_____

3. What were Paul's ultimate criteria for women to pray and prophesy publicly in the Church? How were the same criteria applicable to men? (See *Fashioned to Reign* pages 146, 149.)

_____

_____

_____

4. The Father and Christ Jesus (and the Holy Spirit, for that matter) are equally God but have different roles. Yet Christ subjected Himself to the will of the Father, and God the Father promoted Christ to the highest place. What does that model for men and

women regarding service and sacrifice? (See *Fashioned to Reign* pages 150–151.)

_____

_____

_____

5. According to Hebrews 13:17, all believers are to be in submission to spiritual authority. In what ways can authority from God flow? (See *Fashioned to Reign* page 152.)

_____

_____

_____

Day 4

The Process of Elimination

Desire earnestly spiritual gifts, but especially that you may prophesy. . . . Now I wish that you *all* spoke in tongues, but even more that you would prophesy. . . .

When you assemble, *each one* has a psalm, has a teaching, has a revelation, has a tongue, has an interpretation. Let all things be done for edification.

1 Corinthians 14:1, 5, 26, emphasis added

Sometimes working backward from the usual approach can be a great tool in understanding difficult verses of Scripture. For over a thousand years, brilliant Greek scholars have argued over the meaning of the apostle Paul's much-debated 1 Corinthians passages concerning the role of women and have come to vastly different conclusions. In today's book reading, I try coming from the opposite direction, via the process of elimination. If we can figure out what those complex passages definitely *do not* mean, that puts us that much closer to accurately understanding what they *do* mean.

We have already established in our study that Paul wrote 1 Corinthians to both the men *and* the women in the congregation of Corinth. He had several things he needed to straighten out in their thinking. Coming out of a pagan culture that promoted the worship of numerous and competing deities, the new believers were a little confused by the concept of there being "varieties of gifts, but the same Spirit . . . varieties of ministries, and the same Lord" (1 Corinthians 12:4–5). He had to clarify for them that it was "the same God who works all things in all persons" (verse 6). Another thing he also had to clarify was that he specifically wanted them *all* to desire the spiritual gifts, especially prophecy, and *all* to speak in tongues, and that *each one* would assemble with something to contribute for edification.

By the process of elimination, then, if Paul wanted them *all* to seek and operate in the different gifts and *each one* could contribute to church gatherings, we can eliminate the possibility that women—fully half of the *all*—were to be universally restricted to silence. It seems certain, then, that he did not mean in his "restrictive" verses that women should never speak up in church.

Then what did Paul's restrictions on women mean? We will save that for Day 5 just ahead.

- Today's Scripture reading: 1 Corinthians 12 and 14
- Today's reading from *Fashioned to Reign*: pages 152–157

1. How was it that the Corinthian church had the right experience, but the wrong doctrine concerning the gifts of the Spirit? (See *Fashioned to Reign* pages 153–154.)

2. When talking about earnestly desiring spiritual gifts and seeing them put into operation in the Church, how do we know that Paul was addressing both men *and* women? (See *Fashioned to Reign* page 153.)

3. From Paul's writings, what are some things we already know for sure regarding the role of women in the Corinthian church? (See *Fashioned to Reign* page 156.)

4. What do you think? Does the idea of women being restricted by two verses to absolute silence in the Church (the Corinthian church and/or the Church of today) make sense in light of what we already know?

Day 5

Nonsense! No way! (ἤ)

Was it from you that the word of God first went forth? Or has it come to you only?

1 Corinthians 14:36

We have now looked at Paul's "restrictive" passages, especially 1 Corinthians 14:34–35 about women keeping silent in the church, from a lot of angles. The verse I quote above follows that particular passage and sheds further light on its meaning. How? That is where the Greek "expletive of disassociation" ἤ comes in.

That sounds more complicated than it is, so hang on before you jump ship because I just mentioned Greek grammar. An expletive is an exclamatory word or phrase (sometimes even an obscene one, though not in Paul's case) that is full of emotion. To disassociate from something is to detach from it or distance yourself in an emphatic way, as in wanting to have nothing to do with it. Paul frequently used that little Greek expletive ἤ in his epistles to distance himself from some of the theologically unsound ideas the believers he was writing to had picked up, either from their culture or their former religions or incorrect teaching. Frequently, whenever he asked a rhetorical question in an epistle, he would answer it himself with "ἤ," by which he meant "Nonsense!" or "No way!" or in essence, "I completely and emphatically disassociate with that crazy idea!"

Today's Scripture readings and my list in today's book reading both give you several example of Scriptures in which Paul used ἤ with great fervor to make a point, although we would not know it without specifically studying this construction. He used it frequently throughout 1 Corinthians, a book largely laid out in a question-and-answer format. It is telling that he used ἤ not once, but twice in 1 Corinthians 14:36, which gives us a strong clue that he disagreed with what came just before that little expletive. What am I saying? I will let you read more about that in today's pages from the book. Even though it is all Greek to me, I think it will make sense to you.

I will also let you read a little bit about Joyce and Dave Meyer and Joyce Meyer Ministries. Because of Joyce's voice that speaks forth powerful teaching and encouragement all over the world, the Church is a much stronger, richer place.

- Today's Scripture reading: 1 Corinthians 6; 1 Corinthians 9:1–14
- Today's reading from *Fashioned to Reign*: pages 157–164

1. Did Paul tell anyone else besides women to keep silent in church? Who were they? Were they being told never to talk in a church? What was Paul telling them instead? (See *Fashioned to Reign* page 157.)

2. What was the context of Paul's most restrictive verses in 1 Corinthians 14? What was he trying to accomplish regarding the use of spiritual gifts in meetings and the avoidance of confusion and disruption? (See *Fashioned to Reign* pages 157–158.)

3. Had you ever considered before that much of Paul's writing style in the epistles involved repeating questions believers had and giving his answer? Now that you know more about his style and the Greek grammar behind it, what do you think of the theory many scholars hold that Paul was repeating the men's questions about women in 1 Corinthians 14:34–35 and answering an emphatic ἤ in the verse that followed?

4. All opinions about Paul's "restrictive" verses aside, in what ways was Paul, as a first-century Jewish male and a former Pharisee, a shockingly powerful promoter of women?

_____

_____

_____

5. Joyce and Dave Meyer have completely different yet complementary roles in Joyce Meyer Ministries. The mind-set that women ought not lead or teach in the Church would demand that Joyce and Dave switch roles with each other. What do you think would be the result?

_____

_____

_____

6. I mentioned in the book that in 2005, _Time_ magazine, part of the American news media, acknowledged Joyce Meyer as one of the "25 Most Influential Evangelicals in America." Only three other women were listed, and two of those were mentioned as part of a married couple. What might this say about the Church's stance toward the empowerment of women today?

_____

_____

_____

Session 5 Life Application

Pick out from this session's book readings the verse that you always considered the most restrictive of all the book of Corinthian's verses on women. Quickly write down a few lines about what you always thought that verse meant. Also write down the kind of fallout you have seen in the Church (and possibly in your life, if you are a woman) as a result of that verse and its misapplication.

Now write down a few more lines about how your understanding of that verse has changed since going through this session of *Fashioned to Reign*. Also write down the kind of fallout your new understanding will have as you approach the issue of the empowerment of women in the Church and in society. List some ways in which you will view women and their role differently in the future. List some ways in which you will treat women (and yourself, if you are female) differently.

Session 5 Video Guide

1. Most of the _____ (on women) that we hear about in church and in the Bible come from an apostle who is actually very _____.

2. We all (as Christians) believe in the Bible; the question is, how do we actually _*apply*_ the Bible? It is important not just to know the Word of God, but to know how to apply the right _*word*_ in the right _*Sessions*_.

3. Paul wrote _*13*_ books of the Bible to _____ different cities.

4. When we're talking about the epistles, the letters written to different churches, we're talking about letters written to churches in three separate cultures—the ~~Greek~~ _*Jewish*_ culture, the _*Roman*_ culture and the _*Greek*_ culture.

5. The Greeks believed that women were more _*powerful*_ than men, and so they made _*gods*_ out of women.

6. The only culture Paul wrote anything to that could even seemingly be _*restricted*_ was the _*Greeks*_ culture.

7. The epistles were letters written to _*specific*_ cities about _*S*_ issues.

8. You can't _____ apply a letter written to a specific person about a specific problem.

9. You use _____ to give it away, not to _____ it.

10. Pray that God would release us from the _____ _____ that uses the _____ to oppress people.

A Careful Excavation

I have come to understand that God's plan is not a reaction to the devil's scheme, but quite the opposite! God is not trying to thwart some evil ploy of the enemy; rather, the enemy is reacting to something God has already put in motion. The enemy is on the defense. . . . The enemy is trying to pervert this epic season in which God is empowering His beautiful daughters to sit beside the sons of God and bring wholeness to the nations. The result of this heavy rain will be that sons and *daughters*, fathers and *mothers* will take their rightful seats in heavenly places and begin to move powerfully in celestial unity to destroy the works of the devil.

Fashioned to Reign, page 167

Day 1

Scepters and Thrones

Speaking the truth in love, we are to grow up in all aspects into Him who is the head, even Christ, from whom the whole body, being fitted and held together by what every joint supplies, according to the proper working of each individual part, causes the growth of the body for the building up of itself in love.

Ephesians 4:15–16

A tsunami crashing over the land. Violent winds wreaking havoc. A massive, angry crowd of women shouting in protest. Families torn apart by the chaos in the streets. "Warning! Warning! Warning!" blaring in my mind.

There is nothing pleasant about that scene, yet it was what I saw in my vision on the trip I tell you about in today's reading. It was a representation of the enemy's plan for the country I was in—for any country, I think. The enemy's hope is to stir up a destructive, bitter movement of women acting out against the repression of their sex by rebelling against men.

Then the scene changed. I saw steeples and bells ringing out hope as churches literally emerged from the ground up. This time I envisioned a representation of God's plan, with the men seated on thrones inside the sanctuaries, each man holding a scepter in his hand. Next to each man's throne was a vacant, dusty throne—but not for long! I will let you read the rest of that story in the pages of my book.

My vision started in horror but ended in glory, or at least I thought so. The problem was, God had shared it with me so that I would share it with the male leaders of the conference where I was a guest speaker. Let's just say they were not all fans of my interpretation at the start, particularly their resident theologian. I am thankful that it led to some interesting dialogue between us. I invite you to join us in that dialogue for the rest of this session as we excavate some restrictive foundations together.

- Today's Scripture reading: Ephesians 4:1–16; Proverbs 27:17
- Today's reading from *Fashioned to Reign*: pages 165–169

1. Have you ever met a Christian who seems to enjoy talking endlessly about doom-and-gloom predictions? Why could such a person more appropriately be called a *facter* than a *believer*? (See *Fashioned to Reign* page 166.)

_____

_____

_____

2. Do you remember why the men and women in the vision I shared had different-colored scepters (sapphire for men and ruby for women)? What does that tell us about the call of men and women to lead? (See *Fashioned to Reign* page 167.)

_____

_____

_____

3. Did you ever need to share with someone an insight or a word from the Holy Spirit that you felt might not be well received, as I did at the conference I tell you about in the book? Was it as challenging for you as it was for me? How did you approach it? What was the response?

_____

_____

_____

4. Do you think that after completing this study, you may need to share what you have learned about the empowerment of women in God's Kingdom with some who may not receive it very well? What

will you do to make sure you are not argumentative with them, but rather will speak the truth in love?

_____

_____

_____

Day 2

Theological Bullying

Beloved, while I was making every effort to write you about our common salvation, I felt the necessity to write to you appealing that you contend earnestly for the faith which was once for all handed down to the saints.

Jude 1:3

Nobody likes a bully. Somebody might do what a bully says because in the moment, he or she is coerced into it. But in the long run, no love is lost between them.

Is that how we want it to be between us and those who take a different scriptural position than we do? May the best or the strongest theological bully win? I hope not, yet many of our theological dialogues turn into just that—theological bullying.

How do we contend earnestly for the faith, then, without entering into contention with one another? At first, there was some theological pushing and shoving going on in my "discussion" with those male leaders at the conference I mention in the book. (See what I say in today's pages about the huge difference between the terms *dialogue* and *discussion*.) I felt a little bullied and was tempted to do some bullying myself. It was hard for me to stay calm and not become defensive. (I am guessing that you have been involved in a few of those theological "discussions" yourself.) But I do not want people to be convinced or coerced into a belief just because I say so and I can land more scriptural punches than they can. That method does not bring deep or lasting change.

What changes people is the Word of God illuminated in their hearts by the Spirit of God. None of us can help that process in someone else by theological bullying. It does not work to step beyond the boundaries of our favor with a person or organization in attempting to persuade them of something. What works is honest, respectful dialogue taking place in a way that helps people understand each other's positions through the Scriptures.

I am so glad that after a rocky start, what took place between me and the male leaders of that conference turned into true theological dialogue. They realized that I was doing my best to honor both them and the Scriptures, and I realized that they were doing all they could to both hear me out and be true to God's Word to the best of their understanding. With those realizations came an ability to move forward together to seek God's mind and heart on the issue at hand, the empowerment of female Church leaders in that country.

- Today's Scripture reading: Romans 14:1–12
- Today's reading from *Fashioned to Reign*: pages 169–173

Questions to Consider

1. Based on the Greek words *dia* and *logos* (a two-way flow or exchange of meaning) and the Latin word *discutere* (to strike asunder or break up) that I talk about on page 170, what is your understanding of the difference between a dialogue and a discussion? Which do you tend to enter into when talking with people about theology?

2. Do you find, as I have, that some believers can be okay with applying the historical context of Scripture to define their position in one situation, but then they can completely discount the historical context in another situation? Why do you suppose people do that?

3. We are all, in fact, inclined to read the Bible in a way that validates what we already believe. What is the danger in that tendency, especially in regard to Scriptures taken out of historical context?

Day 3

The Hard Questions

A woman must quietly receive instruction with entire submissiveness. But I do not allow a woman to teach or exercise authority over a man . . .

1 Timothy 2:11–12

At some point, we have to answer the hard questions about the Bible's stance on women. That was one important thing I realized at the conference I told you about in Days 1 and 2 of this session. I walked away from my dialogue with the male leadership that final day knowing I had been ill-prepared to answer their deep theological questions and certain that I needed to do everything in my power to correct that in myself.

With those men of integrity in mind, I took the worst first, so to speak. I began to excavate passages such as 1 Timothy 2:11–15 to their very foundations so that I could understand them better myself and explain the scriptural basis of my understanding to others. That particular passage is one that for centuries has provided the cornerstone of limitations on female leadership in the Church, so it seemed like the right place to start as I sought to understand the scriptural and theological basis of the vision God had given me about the scepters and thrones representing the empowerment of women in the Kingdom.

In today's *Fashioned to Reign* reading, I take you through my archaeological dig into 1 Timothy 2:11–15 in all its detail. I think what I dug up will fascinate you. Take a close look at the findings with me. If you are someone who—either reluctantly or with relish—has applied that passage to restrict and limit women in leadership roles, I believe my excavation will give you a whole new perspective. It certainly gave me one. No longer did I need to pass over such scriptural "trouble spots" and figure that I would have to take the word of someone better and brighter than I am on such passages. It turns out that answering the hard questions is not so hard if we will put forth a little time and effort to do so. As you will discover with me, the results are more than worth our every effort.

- Today's Scripture reading: 1 Timothy 2; 2 Corinthians 9:6–15
- Today's reading from *Fashioned to Reign*: pages 173–179

1. If he was not referring to the salvation of their souls, as so many suppose, then what, exactly, did Paul mean by saying in 1 Timothy 2:15 that women would be preserved (*sozo*) through childbirth? Why was such a statement important to make in light of the Ephesian culture's worship of the goddess Artemis? (See *Fashioned to Reign* pages 175–176.)

_____

_____

_____

2. If he was not referring to women being in submission to men, as so many suppose, then what did Paul mean by saying in 1 Timothy 2:11 that women must receive instruction with entire submissiveness? How does the Greek word for submissiveness, *hupotage*, back up this understanding in context? (See *Fashioned to Reign* pages 176–177.)

_____

_____

_____

3. What is significant about the Greek word *authentein* and its single, solitary use in Scripture (in our passage), compared to the multiple uses of other words in the Bible for taking authority or governing? (See *Fashioned to Reign* pages 177–178.)

_____

_____

_____

4. What do you think of Kroeger and Kroeger's conclusions about the word *authentein*, which I state on page 179?

_____

_____

_____

5. Again, taking into consideration the Ephesian culture's worship of the goddess Artemis, why did it make sense for Paul to say in 1 Timothy 2:12 that a woman must not teach in such a way as to *authentein* (in the Greek) a man?

_____

_____

_____

Day 4

Women in the Ministry?

> On the next day we left and came to Caesarea, and entering the house of Philip the evangelist, who was one of the seven, we stayed with him. Now this man had four virgin daughters who were prophetesses. As we were staying there for some days, a prophet named Agabus came down from Judea. . . .
>
> Acts 21:8–10

Note in the passage above that both women and men were acknowledged as having the title of a prophet (or prophetess, as the case may be) in the New Testament Church. That is important to note. Everyone could prophesy under the infilling of the Spirit (according to Acts 2:17), but not everyone had the governmental office of a prophet (as referred to in Ephesians 4:11–12). There was no reason for the writer of Acts to mention specifically that Philip's daughters were prophetesses unless they were among those who held that title or office in the Church.

This example, along with other instances I give you in today's reading, shows that without question, women were "in the ministry" in the early Church. They were in the ministry long before that, though. I also name several examples of female leaders in the Old Testament. We need to keep these women in mind when we read Paul's "restrictive passages" in his epistles and are tempted to apply them across the board, to all women everywhere, all the time.

We also need to keep in mind, as I mentioned in the previous session and will mention here again, that Paul's concerns about women in the Church were specifically addressed to three cities: Corinth, Ephesus and the island of Crete. Remember that not every first-century church saw every epistle Paul wrote. At times, he suggested that they pass his letters around from church to church. At times, he did not make that suggestion. And you guessed it—Paul never suggested that his epistles containing the "restrictions" on women be passed from church to church. I believe he was intentional about that. Apparently, it was never his intent to go beyond the relevant culture and circumstances with those restrictions. So the question is, why is it ours?

- Today's Scripture reading: Judges 4:4–10; Luke 2:36–38; Romans 16:1–16
- Today's reading from *Fashioned to Reign*: pages 180–185

1. What is the contextual dilemma we face in dealing with the apostle Paul's "restrictive" passages concerning women? (See *Fashioned to Reign* pages 180–181.)

_____

_____

_____

2. Name some ways we know for sure that most women in the first-century Church were not restricted from teaching and having authority in Paul's day. (See *Fashioned to Reign* pages 181–182.)

_____

_____

_____

3. What is the difference between prophesying under the infilling of the Holy Spirit and holding the governmental office of a prophet (or prophetess)? What is that office's job description? (See *Fashioned to Reign* pages 183–184.)

_____

_____

_____

4. What does it take in order for us to both glean from the whole of Paul's epistles and to avoid misapplying the important passages of Scripture we have been talking about?

_____

_____

_____

Day 5

Drawing a Crowd

Whatever you do, do your work heartily, as for the Lord rather than for men, knowing that from the Lord you will receive the reward of the inheritance. It is the Lord Christ whom you serve.

Colossians 3:23–24

By the age of four, Aimee Semple McPherson was already drawing a crowd on street corners with her Bible preaching, and she never stopped. As time went on and her influence increased, they had to call out the National Guard in San Diego to assist with the crowds who came to hear her preach!

You may already know Aimee's story, but if not, I quickly summarize it in today's reading. Her astounding list of achievements would be impressive of anyone, anywhere, anytime, yet the bulk of what she accomplished was done in the 1920s and 1930s—as a *woman*.

With courage and creativity, Aimee shattered the glass ceiling of women in ministry. As you can well imagine, she ran into plenty of doubters and naysayers back then (as she still would today), but she paid them little attention. She kept her focus on what she felt God had called her to do. She knew how to make the most of every opportunity and season her speech with salt so that as many people as possible would hear the Gospel (see Colossians 4:5–6).

As founder of the Foursquare movement, Aimee started a denomination in 1923 that currently numbers 66,000 churches in 140 countries. She also built a Bible college still in existence today, and she wrote 175 songs and hymns, 13 screenplays and several operas. She knew how to use the media and technology of her day to influence people for Christ.

(Not all of us can say as much.) In today's reading, I call Aimee Semple McPherson a princess warrior, a history maker and a forerunner for women all over the world. She was all that and more.

- Today's Scripture reading: Colossians 3
- Today's reading from *Fashioned to Reign*: pages 186–188

Questions to Consider

1. Aimee Semple McPherson was reaching millions all over the world through her radio station and newspaper sermon reprints at a time when women had barely gained the right to vote, much less to lead anything outside the scope of their housework and children. What qualities do you think Aimee had that helped her achieve so much spiritual influence and authority?

_____

_____

_____

2. Thousands upon thousands of people found the Lord through Aimee's entertaining and creative media productions. How can the Church of today follow her example and use cultural media and technology to impact the world for Christ?

_____

_____

_____

3. Here is one of Aimee's more famous quotes: "We are all making a crown for Jesus out of these daily lives of ours, either a crown of golden, divine love, studded with gems of sacrifice and adoration, or a thorny crown, filled with the cruel briars of unbelief, or self-ishness, and sin." Whether you are male or female, how does that thought affect you when you think about reaching your full potential in Christ?

_____

_____

_____

Session 6 Life Application

Ask the Holy Spirit to show you any situations in which you may need to approach another believer or believers who may not be receptive to what you have to say. Whether your topic is the role of women in the Church or something else, how will you make sure that your approach encourages more of a dialogue than a discussion? (Review the difference between those two words on page 170 of the book if needed.) List some ways here to keep your difficult dialogue from turning into an argument. Be specific about how you plan to respond to those who do not see things your way.

Decide now to give other believers who may not think exactly as you do the benefit of the doubt. List a few ways you can think of to do that even in the "heat of conversation." Remember the experience I told you about in this session. Even though the male leaders with whom I discussed my vision were initially opposed to me, I found out that they were not doing it out of some self-serving desire to demean women. They simply had a heart to honor God by walking in the best understanding of Scripture they had. I did my best to show them respect for taking that attitude.

Giving each other more grace in the midst of such dialogues by speaking the truth *in love* is one important way we can promote unity with each other and advance the Kingdom of God together.

Session 6 Video Guide

1. The New Testament ought to be more _____ than the Old Testament where all of us lived under a _____.

2. Sometimes people do not want to look at the _____ of a Scripture because it violates their understanding of what should happen in their _____.

3. Women _____ in Bible days, for example _____ with her husband, Aquila, in Acts 18:26.

4. _____ means to _____ with the back of a hand in 1 Timothy 2.

5. Women and men were _____ to rule and reign _____.

6. God never intended to _____ women or to make them "_____ _____."

7. You cannot apply the epistles the way you would an Old Testament book because the epistles were written to specific _____ to cover specific _____ at specific _____.

Role Reversals

The truth is that the absence of the feminine and matriarchal presence in leadership has come at an incalculable and sometimes cataclysmic expense to society. In the last thirty years, I have observed many women coming into their place in leadership, but . . . for multiple reasons they are often required to play the patriarchal role. This, of course, puts them at a disadvantage because it does not optimize their leadership abilities. It is all too tempting to observe this dynamic and conclude that men are better leaders than women. I would like to propose to you that men are better patriarchs than women and women are stronger matriarchs than men. Both roles are equally important and carry the same level of authority, but they require different skills, strengths and attributes.

We do not need women to lead like men. The world is starving for matriarchs who are compassion driven, intuitively gifted, nurturing leaders. These leaders foster the maternal instinct in society that gives birth to a much more loving, caring, patient and compassionate planet. It is my honest conviction that if women were commissioned to lead in their rightful *place* and *role* globally, the planet would be a much safer, more compassionate, nurturing place to live. Violence and war would dramatically decrease worldwide if women would co-lead *with* men, without feeling the pressure to lead *as* men.

Fashioned to Reign, page 197

Day 1

Gender Profiling

You husbands in the same way, live with your wives in an understanding way, as with someone weaker, since she is a woman.

1 Peter 3:7

We have entered into a lot of discussion about what both Peter and Paul could have meant in their various "restrictive" passages concerning women. How about the verse above? Was Peter doing some serious gender profiling by making the suggestion that women as a gender are less capable, less intelligent or less spiritually attuned than men? I do not think so. I think he simply meant that as a rule, men are physically stronger than women and should not use that strength to take unfair advantage.

These days, you can ask almost anyone if gender profiling is bad, and they will shout a resounding "Yes!" I would have to qualify my affirmative answer to that. Like it or not, there are some obvious and not-so-obvious gender differences built into men and women. I do not think acknowledging those differences is a bad thing. In fact, as I told you back at the beginning, I think men and women are two halves of a whole, and I believe our differences are God-ordained. Those differences add unique strengths to the whole that we would not otherwise have if we were exactly the same as each other.

That is not to say that our differences limit us to certain roles. Not at all. Either a man or a woman can be the powerful CEO of a large corporation. Either a man or a woman can be a caring stay-at-home parent. What I am saying is that men and women will approach the same role differently because of who they are. Or at least, they should be free to approach the same role differently.

That is not always the case, though. What I call "gender cloning" gets in the way, and yes, that is a bad thing. We create a lot of dysfunction on a personal level and in society at large when we expect men to approach certain roles like being a stay-at-home parent the same way a woman would, and when we expect women to approach certain roles like being the CEO of a corporation the same way a man would.

What would happen if we allowed men and women to approach whatever roles God calls them to as *themselves*, with whatever personality characteristics and gender God gave them? In today's reading and in the days ahead in this session, we will look at that idea a little more closely.

- Today's Scripture reading: 1 Peter 3:1–9
- Today's reading from *Fashioned to Reign*: pages 189–193

Questions to Consider

1. I tell you in today's reading about how my youngest son, Jason, was forced to play the dual roles of both father and mother when his first marriage tragically ended. You probably know single parents who have been put in that position, or perhaps you have been there yourself. What are a few of the difficulties someone playing dual gender roles has to face?

2. On page 191 of the book, I make the statement that while gender distinctions should not determine *where* men and women lead, they should make a difference in *how* men and women lead. What kind of freedom could that idea bring to you or someone you know who has been on the receiving end of some gender cloning?

3. How did God synergistically enhance the strength of our gender differences? Along with that, how does He uniquely create each of us to fulfill our divine destinies? (See *Fashioned to Reign* page 192.)

4. What does it do to our proficiency level when we are forced to operate in ways that do not play to our gender's strengths? (See *Fashioned to Reign* page 193.) Give a personal example of this.

_____

_____

_____

Day 2

Sleeping Beauty or G.I. Jane?

Do nothing from selfishness or empty conceit, but with humility of mind regard one another as more important than yourselves; do not merely look out for your own personal interests, but also for the interests of others.

Philippians 2:3–4

*I*t's a man's world out there" goes the well-known saying, and a lot of men believe it. A lot of women believe it, too, and react to it by doing all they can to become like a man. Where the feminine is devalued and women are oppressed, they often embrace the masculine out of a deep desire to feel accepted and equally valued. The result is something I call the G.I. Jane syndrome.

I see nothing wrong with a woman being a strong G.I Jane type if that is who God created her to be. Many woman love to hunt, fish, engage in sports that test their physical prowess and behave in other ways that some cultures identify as typically male. It is not the behavior that causes issues; it is the motivation. As I say in today's reading, if people's actions come out of a whole and healthy personhood, then their passions should be celebrated as part of the personality God gave them.

If, however, those actions are *reactions* to the unhealthy demands of repressive relationships or a prejudiced culture, that is a whole different scenario. Women are forced into becoming G.I. Janes as a way to gain equal footing in a world of inequality.

Sometimes women do just the opposite, though. They become Sleeping Beauties. Feeling crushed in spirit and robbed of their destinies, they react to male dominance by simply giving in. Like Sleeping Beauty, they go to sleep (spiritually and emotionally, anyway), and they yield their influence and authority as princesses of the Kingdom to the men with whom they were meant to rule and reign.

The Sleeping Beauties need to be kissed awake by their Savior and Prince, who has already freed them from the curse. The G.I. Janes need to rest in His assurance that they can be strong Kingdom warriors *and* beautiful Kingdom princesses, knowing that the two are not mutually exclusive.

I would love to see women be free to be who they are—not forced to be who they are not. I believe the God whose very idea it was to create women would love to see the same thing.

- Today's Scripture reading: Philippians 2:1–15; Romans 12:9–21
- Today's reading from *Fashioned to Reign*: pages 193–197

1. Think of a G.I. Jane woman you know. How do you think she became that way? Is her persona a function of a strong and healthy personality? Or is it a reaction to male dominance or unhealthy cultural expectations?

2. Why is competing with men on an equal basis in professional sports or in arenas such as the Olympics likely to result in women being assigned a second-class or "B team" status? How does that kind of competition serve to validate the chauvinistic stance of many men? (See *Fashioned to Reign* pages 194–195.)

3. Why do you think so many women fall into the trap of playing masculine games against men to make the point that they are equally valuable? What are some other ways they might better succeed at making their point?

4. How has the subjugation of women siphoned off the resources men need to fulfill their God-appointed roles? (See *Fashioned to Reign* pages 196–197.)

5. Do you know any women who lead in the strength of their woman-hood, as Tracy Evans does? (I tell you about her grace and courage in today's reading.) What kind of exploits can such a woman do for the Kingdom?

_____

_____

_____

Day 3

Find Your Places, Please

The man gave names to all the cattle, and to the birds of the
sky, and to every beast of the field, but for Adam there was not
found a helper suitable for him. So the LORD God caused a deep
sleep to fall upon the man, and he slept; then He took one of
his ribs and closed up the flesh at that place. The LORD God
fashioned into a woman the rib which He had taken from the
man, and brought her to the man.

Genesis 2:20–22

From the beginning, our Creator purposed in His mind a divine
intent for women. He had a place in mind for women to fill, just
as He had a place in mind for men. If only we would all find
our places, please, the world and the Church would be far better places.

It would not hurt, either, to let others—especially those of the opposite gender—find their God-given places without assigning them a
place where we think they should be. That was always my intent in my
marriage to Kathy, but my childhood experiences made carrying it out
a bit of a challenge. I tell you in today's book pages how my biological
father died when I was three, so I grew up under the influence of a couple
stepfathers who were tyrants at best and cruel and abusive at worst. They
were strong leaders by sheer force, but were unpleasant and unjust—not
in any way attributes that made their family want to relate with them.
Nor did I want to follow their example.

Going into marriage, I respected Kathy's innate wisdom and wanted
her to have a powerful and influential place in our lives. I just was not
sure because of my background how to foster that. I was too busy trying

to understand how her mind worked! It certainly did not travel along the same paths my mind traveled when making decisions. In today's reading, I give you one example of the conversations we would have that would drive me out of my mind. My mind would be working on an *aha* basis—here are the facts; here is our logical decision; eureka, let's do it now! Kathy's mind would be working on an *ah* basis—I feel like we should wait on this . . . *ah* . . . I'm not sure why . . . *ah* . . . let's pray about it for a while.

It took me a while, all right, before I stopped letting my *ahas* railroad Kathy's *ahs* in the direction I wanted to go. It took me awhile to let Kathy find her proper place without pushing her into the position I wanted her in. But I am so glad I finally made that adjustment in my thinking. More about the *ahs* and *ahas* in Day 4 just ahead.

- Today's Scripture reading: Genesis 2:18–25
- Today's reading from *Fashioned to Reign*: pages 198–203

Questions to Consider

1. Why is it significant that the Hebrew word *tesla*, often translated "rib" in Genesis 2, is usually translated "side chamber" according to several other occurrences in Scripture? How does that help define the relationship between men and women? (See *Fashioned to Reign* pages 198–199.)

2. What does it mean to say that a woman processes things from the heart to the head, whereas a man processes things from the head to the heart? Can you give an example from your own experience of either processing method?

3. Although violence toward women is not tolerated within church walls, what happens when the devaluation of women is "spiritualized" in the Church? (See *Fashioned to Reign* pages 200–201.)

Day 4

The *Ahs* and the *Ahas*

Now faith is the assurance of things hoped for, the conviction of things not seen. . . . And without faith it is impossible to please Him.

Hebrews 11:1, 6

*I*t actually simplified things for me when I finally figured out that my wife's *ahs* had multiple meanings. It was definitely one of my brightest *aha* moments when I realized that Kathy's *ah* was not so much about what she was thinking as about how she was thinking. Her *ah* meant that she was feeling her way through a situation in a way I likely never would or could, and she was grasping something about it intuitively that would give us valuable insight or direction. For a guy full of a Spocklike need for logic and order, that was a little hard to grasp.

A woman's ability to grasp the intricacies of a problem and come up with a solution often goes beyond logic or reason. This is why we men need some *aha* moments in our conversations with the ladies. It is also why women tend to more easily embrace the higher realms of the Kingdom—the realms entered into by faith, not by sight. And it is why, as I travel the world to equip churches in prophetic ministry, I find it interesting but not surprising that everywhere I go, 75 to 80 percent of those who gather as intercessors or prophetic people are women. Men tend to neutralize their spiritual connectivity by focusing on the facts and the laws of physics. Women tend to accept and value things that are inexplicable in the halls of science. Moving in the prophetic therefore comes more naturally to women.

Because of that, and because of the unique strengths and gender distinctions of men and women, we would see a lot more balance in the Church if matriarchs were empowered to take their proper place alongside the patriarchs who have ruled the Church for centuries. We would also see our ability to reach the world skyrocket. It is past time for us to set things right.

- Today's Scripture reading: 2 Corinthians 5:7; Hebrews 11:1–6
- Today's reading from *Fashioned to Reign*: pages 203–205

——— *Questions to Consider* ———

1. Whatever your gender, have you ever run into a conflict between the *ahs* of women and the *ahas* of men? How did you work through it?

2. The Hollywood entertainment industry certainly recognizes gender preferences. Think about the proliferation of "chick flicks" versus "man movies." Why does that kind of profiling actually make some sense in light of our gender distinctions? (See *Fashioned to Reign* page 204.)

3. Has your observation of intercessors and prophetic people yielded the same percentages of men and women as mine? If yes, how might men do a better job of developing and enhancing their spiritual connectivity and sensitivity?

Day 5

Rock the Cradle

For I am convinced that neither death, nor life, nor angels, nor principalities, nor things present, nor things to come, nor powers, nor height, nor depth, nor any other created thing, will be able to separate us from the love of God, which is in Christ Jesus our Lord.

Romans 8:38–39

Women can change the world in countless ways, but one way in particular leaves a lasting legacy. Rocking the cradle and raising a child who loves and serves the Lord is an often overlooked way to make and change history. Sarah Edwards, whose story I briefly detail in today's reading, raised eleven children to do just that.

Sarah was born the daughter of a minister in 1710, and she became the wife of preacher and theologian Jonathan Edwards only seventeen years later. By 1900, Sarah and Jonathan's descendants included numerous college presidents, professors, lawyers, judges, physicians, public servants, and undoubtedly numerous loving mothers determined to rock the cradle and influence the world.

Mothering was far from the only thing that occupied Sarah Edwards, as you will see in my brief biography of her in the book. But mothering was something she made a top priority. Working in and around her busy husband and household, Sarah prayed constantly for her children. Her prayer life was legendary. She also diligently taught her children the Word of God. She poured much of her life into raising them for the Lord, making an investment in them that continued to pay off in their progeny for generations (according to a study of their more than fourteen hundred descendants).

Devoted, determined mothers are some of the strongest, most influential women in the world. We will revisit that fact in the next session. Keep Sarah Edwards in mind as a prime example when we do.

- Today's Scripture reading: Romans 8:35–39 (said to be Sarah's favorite passage)
- Today's reading from *Fashioned to Reign*: pages 206–208

Questions to Consider

1. Even though during her lifetime, Sarah Edwards was not a well-known personality, a public speaker or a preacher, her life has impacted American society for centuries. How did she manage it?

2. For a long time, American culture has devalued the contribution and importance of mothering. Do you think that is changing at all? If so, how? If you are not from America, what value does your culture place on motherhood, high or low?

3. What kind of hope and encouragement does Sarah's story give the mothers of today?

Session 7 Life Application

We talked in this session about how gender profiling is not necessarily always a bad thing if it is simply an acknowledgment of the God-given differences between the genders, but gender cloning is always harmful. Gender cloning demands that one gender approach things the same exact way as the other to be considered effective or capable. That expectation is both unfair and impossible.

Think about a situation in which you feel you are on the receiving end of some gender cloning. (Both men and women can be on the receiving end.) What are your frustrations in that situation? What are your prayers about it? What is your forgiveness level toward those responsible?

How would you approach things differently if you were allowed to do things according to your own strengths and not according to someone else's expectations? Ask the Holy Spirit to give you insight into how you might work toward improving the situation. Pray for favor with those whose expectations are misguided, and pray for opportunities to show your God-given strengths and leadership abilities.

Session 7 Video Guide

1. The strength that it takes to be something you're not _____ off the _____ you have to be what you are.

2. Some male leaders are _afraid_ of women and don't _understand_ them. You tend to _control_ what you don't understand.

3. Society totally lost _value_ for the _matriarcl_ side of God and of women.

4. God's invisible _attributes_ His eternal _power_ and divine _nature_ are clearly seen in what God made.

5. God never causes us to _operate_ outside of who we are. He just says, "_Be you_ ."

6. We're not looking for women to be _dominant_ or men to be _dominant_, we're looking for _permission_ to be us in any environment.

7. You'll never achieve _excellence_ as a leader when you try to be somebody and something that you're _not_ .

8. Women were made to lead as _women_, not as _man_ .

9. You can't just marry; you have to _merge_ .

10. The word _suitable_ means _corresponding_ to or _opposite_ of.

11. If you want to make good decisions, you need the _patriarch_ and the _matriarch_.

Powerful Diversity

A strong woman is someone who is walking in her God-given identity, unaffected by the world's image of the feminine role or the religious pressure to conform to some reduced version of herself. There is so much peer pressure in the world for people to become a copy of someone else instead of being an original of themselves.

Fashioned to Reign, page 221

Day 1

The Strong, Silent Type

Your adornment must not be merely external—braiding the hair, and wearing gold jewelry, or putting on dresses; but let it be the hidden person of the heart, with the imperishable quality of a gentle and quiet spirit, which is precious in the sight of God.

1 Peter 3:3–4

Strong is not always defined as extroverted, driven or dominant. Sometimes there is a quiet strength that stays in the background, unheralded and unobtrusive, but packed with power. Think about the term *gentle giant* and all it implies. Many women I know are gentle giants in the spirit. They are strong, silent types who serve behind the scenes, but who are worthy of just as much honor as those living in the limelight.

Kathy was the strong, silent type for much of our marriage. I cannot even begin to describe the numerous ways in which she provided strength and stability for me and our family in the midst of some difficult times. While her role has been changing as she has stepped up to serve the Church in teaching and administrative capacities, it was she who reminded me, as I was writing *Fashioned to Reign*, not to forget that empowered women fit many different descriptions. She reminded me that it would do a disservice to my topic to give the impression that all strong women are D personality leaders taking the world by storm. Certainly, some empowered women fit that description. Others fit the description of a godly, stay-at-home wife and mother who rocks the cradle and rules the world, as we saw in Sarah Edwards at the end of Session 7.

One description a strong woman should *not* fit is difficult and disrespectful. As I tell you in today's book reading, some women I have overseen in the workplace or in ministry were full of bad attitudes toward men. Talk about gender profiling! Whenever I refused to accept their insubordination, they would pull the "woman card" on me and accuse me of chauvinism because I would not put up with their rebelliousness. I see no reason to put up with a rebellious woman any more than I would put up with a rebellious man!

I do realize, however, that some of these women are fighting what I call the "ghost syndrome," which makes them much more highly sensitized to anything that they perceive as male chauvinism. The problem is in their perceptions. Because of hurts or abusive experiences of the past, they tend to see anything a man says or does as insulting, even when no insult was intended. I give you one example of that in the book, and I also talk more about what triggers the ghost syndrome and how it can be overcome.

- Today's Scripture reading: Mark 9:33–37
- Today's reading from *Fashioned to Reign*: pages 209–214

Questions to Consider

1. Whether male or female, are you more of a strong, silent type providing stability and support in the background, or are you more of a D personality, "let me lead and you follow" type person? How do you see your personality type fitting in with God's divine destiny for you?

   Strong silent type providing stability and support. I'm to continue being strong silent helping people

2. Kathy began our marriage as the strong, in-the-background person, but eventually changed to more of a leader in the limelight as God called her to serve in new and different ways. Describe how you or someone you know has also changed roles (either the way Kathy did or in the opposite direction) on the journey toward fulfilling God's plan and purpose in his or her life.

   God had me join Carol in her ministry and I'm still doing it with friends struggling being a Christian

3. Have you met any women who automatically feel entitled to be disrespectful or insubordinate because in the past they or other women have been oppressed, so they are bound and determined to avoid it? How does that have the opposite effect of the one they intend because it perpetuates gender incongruity? (See *Fashioned to Reign* page 211.)

   Yes, she had to fight everything she didn't like or didn't understand

4. Now that you have read my description of the "ghost syndrome," do you think you have ever experienced it in yourself? Or have you ever met anyone (male or female) who seems to suffer from it? What

are some redemptive ways you can think of that such ghosts can be put to rest?

I have experienced when I first became a Christian. It can be put to Rest when you turn to God and have faith trust n belief, he will help you thru it.

Day 2

Elevating Motherhood

My son, observe the commandment of your father
And do not forsake the teaching of your mother.

Proverbs 6:20

I hope you know by now that I am not someone who wants to legislate which gender stays at home to raise the children and which gender goes forth into the workplace to "bring home the bacon." Women must fulfill their God-given commission to co-reign alongside men in whatever role God directs them to play.

I am, however, someone who wants to elevate the call to motherhood. For a long time, the trend in American society has been to devalue motherhood. What massive gender confusion this has caused! It is a trend we *must* turn around for the sake of our children and our children's children. It is a scientific fact that most of our core beliefs about love and security are formed in our first four years of life. The importance of a mother's nurture and influence during that tender time cannot be overestimated. The problem is, our society tends to vastly underestimate it.

The far-reaching effects of motherhood are brilliantly detailed in the poem I included in today's pages of *Fashioned to Reign*. The author of the poem, Christianna Maas, has an amazing grasp on the depth and breadth of a mother's purpose and power. I think her poem will inspire you, as it did me, to realize just how divine a call it is to carry and grow a life, to protect it and nurture it, to teach it and train it, and to love it.

Whatever a woman's personality profile or other roles in the Kingdom, the honor due her as a mother does not change.

- Today's Scripture reading: Psalm 31; Proverbs 6:20–23
- Today's reading from *Fashioned to Reign*: pages 214–221

1. What effects has cloning the sexes in the name of equality had on American society and on our children? If you are not from my country, have you seen it happen in your society as well, and with what effects? (See *Fashioned to Reign* page 215.)

   It has caused untold sickness and reason for growth of homosexuality all over the world.

2. Why do you think so many people equate the promotion of motherhood with the disempowering of women? Is motherhood a lesser call than a career job for women? If so, why is that? Or why do people think so?

   People feel motherhood is disempowering women

3. What was your reaction to Christianna Maas's poem "Motherhood" in today's reading? Which lines or phrases affected you the most profoundly?

   She is a strong woman and a warrior giving life and protecting and nourishing it. Because I smiled instead of frowned the world will know the power of grace.

4. In Proverbs 31, Bathsheba had much to teach her son about marriage. Were the traits she described as desirous in a wife dependent on personality or character? How so? (See *Fashioned to Reign* pages 220–221.)

   On character she puts everything and everyone before herself.

Day 3

The Misunderstood Apostles

Be subject to one another in the fear of Christ.

Ephesians 5:21

*I*t seems as if there is no letup from the relentless pressure the world and the Church bring to bear on women to be someone they are not. It is like those mall mannequins I tell you about in today's book reading. I saw those Westernized mannequins in a place where the women of that country had no hope of ever looking anything like them. The presence of the mannequins fostered an unrealistic expectation that not a single woman there could fulfill. The unfairness of it frustrated me.

The same thing holds true when people use the Bible to manipulate others into doing their will. That frustrates me, too, and we see it every day when it comes to the lack of empowerment of women in the Church. When people apply the Scriptures in an unredemptive way, they miss one of the main points of the Gospel—that Jesus came to bring life abundant.

Think about Peter and Paul and their instructions about marriage. We have spent much of this study talking about their "restrictive" passages concerning women, and those passages turned out to be far less restrictive than most male leaders in the Church would have us believe. Likewise, these two apostles' passages on marriage have been used to restrict and repress wives, which was never the intent. You will see what I mean as we dig into those passages a little bit in today's reading.

If we would all submit ourselves to the Word of God and to each other in the fear of Christ, we would see bondages broken and life abundant flow. We would see the women of the Kingdom fully empowered to walk in their God-given identities, the way He meant for them to do. Let's not try to make over the women God created and designed into someone they are not.

- Today's Scripture reading: 1 Peter 2:13–25; Genesis 18:1–15; 1 Samuel 25
- Today's reading from *Fashioned to Reign*: pages 221–232

Questions to Consider

1. I talk in the book about an unbelieving husband who came to me for counsel, hoping I would help him use Scriptures on marriage to force his wife to behave differently toward him. How was he reading the Bible "like a lawyer, not a lover"? (See *Fashioned to Reign* page 224.)

   like a lawyer.

2. According to Paul in Ephesians 5, how is the headship of a husband about servanthood in motion? Why do you think that servanthood part of his famous marriage passage gets so deemphasized, while the part about wives being subject to their husbands gets so over-emphasized? (See *Fashioned to Reign* pages 225–226.)

3. What was the cultural and historical backdrop of Peter's first epistle? How are those factors significant when it comes to his exhortations to wives in 1 Peter 3:1–6? (See *Fashioned to Reign* pages 229–230.)

4. In 1 Peter 3:5–6 Peter holds up Abraham's wife, Sarah, as an example to godly wives. How does Sarah exemplify both submissiveness and strength? (See *Fashioned to Reign* pages 230–232.)

   She finally Realized who God Really is and his Power and love.

5. When it comes to submission, submitting to God's righteousness often means standing up in boldness against those who would demand that we submit to them and their unrighteous ways instead. How was Abigail in the Old Testament a significant example of this? (See *Fashioned to Reign* page 232.)

She didn't submit to her husban and fed David's men and honored by God

Day 4

The King's Daughters

He who finds a wife finds a good thing
And obtains favor from the LORD.

Proverbs 18:22

Few among us rub shoulders with royalty, but what if we did? What if you knew the king of a vast and powerful kingdom personally? What if in exchange, the king knew everything about you—what you do for a living, where you live and what kind of person you are? And what if he expected that his daughters would be safe around you? What if he trusted that you would treat his precious princesses with respect and honor? Would you ever violate that trust?

You would violate it to your own peril! If you even thought of treating the king's precious girls with anything less than the respect they deserved, he would find you and set you straight mighty quick. And if you actually abused a princess, heaven forbid, there would be nowhere in all of the kingdom or outside it that you could hide from the retribution headed your way.

You do know royalty. Each and every person on this planet was created by a loving heavenly Father who is King of the universe. Each woman and each girl you know is an inconceivably precious princess in her Father's sight. And heaven does forbid their mistreatment at the hands of abusive or ignorant men. Abusers and oppressors dishonor the Lord Almighty's daughters, and there will be nowhere to hide from Him when judgment for such action falls.

I talk a little in today's reading about how enduring abuse is not in any way an expression of covenant love, as some mistakenly suppose. A woman (or a man, for that matter) is under no spiritual obligation to stay in an abusive situation. It is a distortion of the Gospel to insist otherwise.

On the other hand, when you treat the King's daughters with the honor and respect they deserve, you improve your standing with the King. That is why I tell men that if they want to improve their relationship with God, they should marry a King's daughter and treat her like the precious jewel that she is. The beauty of a woman's spirit is like a magnet that attracts the favor of God. We men need women alongside us in more ways than I can count. Truly, women are fashioned to reign.

- Today's Scripture reading: Ephesians 4:25–32
- Today's reading from *Fashioned to Reign*: pages 232–235

1. Why do you think religion tends to demand that a wife in an abusive situation endure the abuse as part of her "submission"? Why is that kind of thinking false religion? (See *Fashioned to Reign* pages 232–233.)

   People believed Jesus wanted them to stay in an abusive marriage because he also said not to stay in a bad marriage

2. On one extreme, spouses with low self-respect and a martyr complex stay in an abusive situation long beyond any efforts toward resolution that God would require of them. On the other extreme, spouses with a low commitment level who are looking for an excuse to walk away will call any conflict "dangerous abuse" and use it as their ticket out. How are both extremes distortions of the Gospel?

   There is no room in the Bible for abuse. Both are distortions

3. We have seen from Scripture and our study that without question, women have been fashioned to reign alongside men. What characteristics do you see in women that are absolutely essential in nurturing this ailing planet back to health?

   Compassion, love, trust, caring

Day 5

Five Fantastic Females

For even as the body is one and yet has many members, and all the members of the body, though they are many, are one body, so also is Christ. . . . Now you are Christ's body, and individually members of it.

1 Corinthians 12:12, 27

*T*here is powerful, and then there is powerful, and then there is powerful . . .

The term *powerful* has a lot of dimensions to it. The concept of being powerful can mean so many things. For that reason, when people who knew I was writing this book would ask me what a powerful woman looks like, I could not give them just one standard answer. There is not just one answer; there are many.

In today's reading from *Fashioned to Reign*, I give you five answers to that very question. They come in the form of some short, descriptive paragraphs about five fantastic females whom I know personally. The women are Beni Johnson, Sheri Silk, Kathy Vallotton, Heidi Baker and Inese Šlesere. Each of these ladies exemplifies a powerful woman walking out her God-given destiny freely and fully. Each is an impressive and empowered feminine leader completely unique and different from the other four. I trust that my descriptions of these ladies will begin to round out for you the concept of a powerful woman.

There is great diversity in the strengths of womanhood. I am sure that along with the five wonderful lady leaders whom I describe, you could add several more whom you know personally. I could have added a hundred more fantastic female leaders if time and space allowed. That is how diverse the roles, personalities and leadership styles of powerful women are.

Strength comes in many packages. Women are beautiful, diverse people who exemplify the feminine side of God. Whether male or female, in fact, each of us on this planet is a one-of-a-kind original designed by our heavenly Father to fulfill His plans and purposes for us. My prayer is that as we walk with and help each other along the way, we would revolutionize how the world and the Church view the women among us who need to be empowered to step into their rightful role as daughters of the King.

- Today's Scripture reading: 1 Corinthians 12:12–27
- Today's reading from *Fashioned to Reign*: pages 237–241

── Questions to Consider ──

1. In your eyes, what are some of the various dimensions of the term *powerful*? How are some of the empowered women you know living examples of the feminine side of God?

   loving caring Strong, leader

2. In Beni Johnson, I give you an example of a powerful woman who is introverted and soft-spoken. Can you think of such a lady whom you know? How is it that being powerful, yet being soft-spoken and gentle can work together in such a personality?

   what they say

3. Sheri Silk is my example of an assertive, outspoken leader. Do you know a female leader with that personality type? Why do you think such personalities can act as powerful voices for the weak and disenfranchised?

   They can say things that get the weaks attention to listen.

4. I have told you more than one story about my wife, Kathy, during this study. She is my example of stability and resourcefulness. One of Kathy's greatest strengths lies in her ability to bring peace into chaotic situations. Whom do you know with that ability? How can a peaceful spirit and powerfulness make such good allies?

   what you say and how you say it.

5. Heidi Baker combines massive intelligence and farseeing vision with great humility and adaptability. She is equally at home spreading the Good News while sitting in a hut or sitting in a mansion. Are you comfortable spreading the Good News in various situations? Why is such adaptability a huge asset in fulfilling the Great Commission?

You must be comfortable wherever you are to spread the good news. humility & adaptability

6. As a wife, mother and politician, Inese Šlesere is in the forefront both on the home front and in her culture at large, through the political arena. Because of her compassion for everyone she meets, atheists listen to her and members of the opposing political party love her. Do you know any feminine leaders whose influence seems to flow out of their compassion for people? How does showing compassion increase their power to reach the world with the Gospel?

A lady at work at Green Pastures showed compassion to the boys and they saw this compassion and the shine in her eyes from Jesus. she also testified to them

Session 8 Life Application

I talked a lot in this session about the different dimensions of being powerful, and I gave you some examples from a very diverse group of powerful women whom I know. They all display different aspects of being empowered to live out their full destinies in Christ. Take a few minutes to list five different dimensions of powerful that you see in them or in others that go beyond the typical take-charge, D personality leader. Now, ask the Holy Spirit to show you if any of the dimensions you listed apply to you (whether you are male or female). Also ask the Spirit if there are other things you could put on the list that would describe you personally. Let God show you the ways in which He has empowered *you* to "be all you can be" in Christ.

With that in mind, also take time right now to seek the Lord about whether anything is hindering you from fulfilling your destiny in Him. Are there past experiences that have left you with the "ghost syndrome" that we talked about in Day 1? Turn them over to God and seek healing so that you can move forward. Or are you trying to fulfill other people's expectations of you when your focus should be on God's expectations? Ask the Lord to sharpen your discernment to know which is which.

Do you need to expand your definition of *powerful* to include more dimensions than you were aware of before? Ask the Lord to help you step out into new and unique realms of leadership that had not occurred to you before this study. Every man and woman on the planet was created by God to fulfill a specific destiny in which he or she plays an important part in bringing the Kingdom to earth. And together, men and women have been formed and fashioned to co-reign.

compassion, soft spoken, assertive, stability & resourcefulness, adaptability

Session 8 Video Guide

1. Heidi Baker's strategy is just to talk to _____ minute by minute.

2. Tracy Evans is the _____ person—not woman, but *person*—Kris knows.

3. Beni Johnson shows that there is something _____ about being who you want to be in Christ, not who other people want you to be.

4. When we, especially as women, know who God _____ us to be, we act out of that and we _____ out of that.

5. The enemy always tries to _____ that and to tell us that we're _____ than that.

6. God showed Kathy Vallotton that to be beautiful means to be _____ until you're _____ of everything that He has placed inside you.

Video Guide
Answer Key

Session 1

1. male, female, image, likeness

2. oppress, revelation

3. represent

4. side chamber

5. fashioned

6. formed, fashioned

Session 2

1. hostility

2. serpent, hostile

3. spiritual warfare, women

4. reduce, reduce

5. husband, men

6. co-reigned

7. woman, complete, taken out

8. brilliant, listened, influenced

9. valid, appropriate

10. right thing, wrong thing, free

11. broke, curse

12. better place, re-create

Session 3

1. letter, Spirit
2. devil, true
3. Spirit
4. wisest, relationship, wisest, loses
5. application, directed
6. leads, truth
7. process, lens
8. tension
9. documentary, commentary, story
10. oppressed, made

Session 4

1. Moses, three, one hundred
2. wives, husbands, men, women
3. burn, teach
4. illegal
5. free, women
6. leadership, passion
7. weeping, weep, understand
8. passionate, emotional, intelligent

Session 5

1. restrictions, empowering
2. apply, word, season
3. thirteen, nine
4. Jewish, Roman, Greek
5. powerful, gods
6. restrictive, Greek
7. specific, specific
8. universally
9. authority, keep
10. religious spirit, Bible

Session 6

1. empowering, curse
2. context, churches
3. taught, Priscilla
4. Authority, slap
5. created, together
6. belittle, less than
7. people, issues, times

Session 7

1. siphons, energy

2. afraid, understand, control

3. value, matriarchal

4. attributes, power, nature

5. operate, "Be you"

6. dominant, dominant, permission

7. excellence, not

8. women, men

9. merge

10. corresponding, opposite

11. patriarch, matriarch

Session 8

1. Jesus

2. bravest

3. powerful

4. created, minister

5. stifle, less

6. you, full

Kris Vallotton has been happily married to his wife, Kathy, since 1975. They have four children and eight grandchildren. Three of their children are in full-time vocational ministry. Kris is the co-founder and senior overseer of the *Bethel School of Supernatural Ministry*, which has grown to more than two thousand full-time students per year. He is also the founder and president of Moral Revolution, an organization dedicated to cultural transformation.

Kris is the senior associate leader of Bethel Church in Redding, California, and has served with Bill Johnson for more than 36 years. He has written and co-authored numerous books, and his revelatory insight and humorous delivery make him a much-sought-after international conference speaker.

You can contact Kris or find out more about his other ministry materials at www.kvministries.com, or you can follow Kris and Kathy on their Facebook fan page at www.facebook.com/kvministries.